Pause

"Elizabeth Caldwell's small, soulful volume is like a prism through which the gentle and passionate light of God reflects through selected psalms. Each chapter invites readers to pause and linger with the ancient words, through a variety of translations and paraphrases, in order that the words can help us uncover layer after layer of personal meaning. Like a relationship that ripens with time, Caldwell's pastoral heart and invitational style gives us a trustworthy companion for our Lenten journeys. Pausing in this way is indeed, as the author states, countercultural. It is also a gift. This book is one I will return to year after year."

—**Eugenia Anne Gamble,** pastor and author of *Words of Love: A Healing Journey with the Ten Commandments*

"While Elizabeth Caldwell has done all the research and provides guidance for individuals as well as lesson plans for groups, her invitation is open and gentle, compelling, not burdensome. She invites us to join the long line of pilgrims who have turned to the Psalms to find their way into God's presence. She is a trustworthy leader for a Lenten pilgrimage that will change your life."

—**Laura Mendenhall,** President Emerita, Columbia Theological Seminary

"In a hurried, often reactive society, 'pausing is truly countercultural,' writes Elizabeth Caldwell. Rich with scriptural voices, personal stories, wise insights, spiritual practices, and teaching tools, *Pause: Spending Lent with the Psalms* is a holy handbook that will help you take a breath, take a break, and find rest for your soul."

—**Rachel M. Srubas,** pastor, spiritual director, and author of *The Desert of Compassion: Devotions for the Lenten Journey*

"From time to time, the Holy Spirit helps me see something in a new way. In this beautiful, thoughtful book, Caldwell helps me see the season of Lent and the Psalms anew. With wisdom and grace, she invites us to open our eyes and tend to our hearts and pause so that God may do what God does best—draw us near and make us more faithful. I am deeply grateful."

—**Rodger Y. Nishioka,** Senior Pastor, Village Presbyterian Church, Prairie Village, Kansas

"In a world of unwelcomed interruptions that leave us stressed out and exhausted, this book invites us to make intentional interruptions in our routine—weekly or daily pauses—as a path to find relaxation and refreshment. May these pauses lead us to more faithful living during Lent and beyond, and may they help us to renew our commitment to build a world where everyone is allowed to pause."

—**Magdalena I. García,** pastor in Chicago and freelance writer

"Caldwell invites readers into the riches of biblical poetry through close reading of the Psalms and furthers that invitation to include stepping out of the ever-increasing pace of our modern world to intentionally pause during the season of Lent. Including spiritual practices both ancient and modern, Caldwell introduces readers to practical activities that can help Christians grow closer to the Divine. *Pause* is an immersion in divine poetry, while also being an excellent resource for personal devotions or small group studies during the Lenten season."

—**Kara Eidson,** pastor and author of *Stay Awhile: Advent Lessons in Divine Hospitality* and *A Time to Grow: Lenten Lessons from the Garden to the Table*

"Renew your faith journey. Listen to the Psalms. Elizabeth Caldwell guides us to drink deep of the wisdom of the Psalms. She invites us to attend to the text, probe its meaning in light of our lives, and connect with God's call. Honoring with integrity the meanings of the Psalms, she draws us into their power to transform us as we move through the season of Lent."

—**Jack L. Seymour,** Professor Emeritus of Religious Education, Garrett-Evangelical Theological Seminary

Pause

Spending Lent with the Psalms

ELIZABETH F. CALDWELL

WESTMINSTER
JOHN KNOX PRESS
LOUISVILLE • KENTUCKY

With thanks to dear friends who listened, read,
and helped me bring these words to life.
For my siblings, Bill, Andy, and Cathy, and their families,
who surround me with the music of their lives,
their faith, and their abiding love.

Contents

Introduction

Consider these words:

running to the next thing
　　to-do list
　　　　pause
　　　　　　interruption
　　　　　　　　wait for it
　　　　　　　　　　slow down
　　　　　　　　　　　　keep going
　　　　　　　　　　　　　　stop

Which of these define the pace of your daily life, either by describing your current reality or expressing what you most need?

Lent is the season of the church year that follows Advent, Christmas, and Epiphany. While Advent invites us to prepare, to wait to receive again the gift of God taking human form in the birth of Jesus, the season of Lent offers a different invitation: one of pausing and observing, reflecting on our lives as Christians. As we engage with the Gospel texts in worship, which tell the stories of Jesus' journey with his followers—stories of teaching and healing, parables and miracles, invitation and challenge—we are invited to enter into this path of discipleship by embarking on the Lenten journey for forty days.

Perhaps you grew up experiencing this season as one of repentance, fasting, and preparing for Holy Week. You may be familiar with the practice of giving up something for Lent, fasting from something you really like. This practice of fasting helps some people to connect with Jesus' life of sacrificial love and his invitation to follow him and do as he does, choosing to live in response to his teaching by practicing surrender.

In addition to the practice of fasting as giving up, there is also a Lenten practice of *taking* up. This can work well for individuals or families with children who are looking for a way to engage thoughtfully and practically with the Lenten season by finding something new and creative to do for forty days—like being especially aware of taking care of the environment or adopting a weekly practice of sharing bread or cookies with a church member or neighbor they don't see very much. One practice I take up during each week of Lent is to have a phone call or video chat with a friend or family member whom I don't see very often. After receiving ashes, I begin making a list of these people on Ash Wednesday. Including these friends and family in my weekly prayers also provides a centering practice for me during Lent. Rather than subtracting something, this practice of addition can be deeply meaningful during Lent—finding ways to turn your attention to a new form of practical service or toward a creative outlet. You may find combining the two practices to be helpful.

Maybe you are well versed in both of these Lenten practices. Or maybe you have little experience with this season of the church year and wonder what it's all about.

The intention of taking up something new usually helps me the most to move through Lent thoughtfully. But sometimes it can become another overly ambitious to-do list. I have a stack of multicolored paper I use for my at-home task list. I'm always adding more things that need to get done during the week. When I was working full-time, the list of things to do usually had to wait for a weekend. "Always busy" would be the label for me—always planning and thinking ahead, always focused on the next thing to get done on my list.

One Lent I decided I wanted to be really focused with a spiritual discipline that I would follow beginning with Ash Wednesday, moving through Lent and Holy Week. I selected two practices, the first involving the online devotional D365 (D365.org), which has original music as background for focusing on a biblical text, reflecting, and praying. It is still one of my favorites. To this I added a practice of following the daily lectionary during Lent. A reading from the Old Testament, another from the New Testament, and a psalm are provided for each day. And so I began. After the third day, I gave up. I realized I was just trying to get through the three lectionary readings. It felt like a race, and I wasn't getting to the finish line—as with so many other things on my to-do list. It was too much, and it just wasn't working for me. So I paused and decided to start over by listening to the online devotional and reading only the psalm for each day. It worked! And it made me think that maybe one can *take* up a new practice in Lent by *giving* up—by doing less.

That's what this book aims to help you do on your Lenten journey. Are you a busy parent who can barely find any time for your spiritual life? Are you retired and now have more time, leaving you with choices about how you will use the hours in each day, or are you busier than ever with social events and volunteering? Are you someone who is seeking a way to move through Lent faithfully, whether or not you've tried this before?

The culture in which we are embedded doesn't invite or encourage us to pause, to lay aside our perpetual activity. It values adaptability to constant change. It requires immediate and constant attention. It expects rapid response. Our connection to devices has, of course, intensified these demands. Meals and even conversations are interrupted with the dinging of a text message that must be read immediately—now, not later! It seems that we are always rushing to the next thing. Pausing is truly countercultural.

The season of Lent offers a limited time frame for taking up a spiritual practice that can help you to focus more deeply on your life of faith, the convictions and the questions that you sense are emerging, by slowing down and being present. We know from research that brains can respond to the many demands for their attention for only so long before a break is required, a space of refreshment. Just as Jesus needed to get away at times to pray, so, too, do his followers, especially in a world requiring our attention in so many different directions. Think of Lent as a refreshing pause in your life to nourish your soul.

So what is your intention for Lent this year? Do you feel drawn to taking something up by doing less? While many resources for Lent lead readers through stories about Jesus from the Gospels, this book is different. It invites you to pause and engage with the Psalms, either individually or with a small group in your church or community, just as countless worshipers and people of faith have done before us—ancient Israelites on pilgrimage to Jerusalem or in the temple, monks in monasteries, and Christian churchgoers of every denomination over the centuries. We will be drawing on that rich meditative tradition to mark these forty days with a simple practice of reading and reflecting with just one psalm each week or holy day, beginning with Ash Wednesday and continuing through the five weeks of Lent and the days of Holy Week, which include Palm Sunday, Maundy Thursday, Good Friday, and Easter. The psalms that you will read and learn about have been selected from those that are read in the Revised Common Lectionary (Years A, B, and C) and heard in worship by many Christian congregations, so you may also hear them read in worship services.

As you read the psalm of the week or of the day, you'll begin to see how an ancient poem/hymn can connect with your own life and circumstances. Interpretive background work will help you attend to the form, meanings, and translations of the psalm, as well as what it reveals about the psalmist and the psalmist's beliefs about God. One thing to note about these psalms you will be reading is that many of them are ascribed to David. Scholars do not think David is their actual author, though at times they do speak to circumstances in the narrative of his life. One way to think about this collection of hymns is that David is the sponsor, "the royal figure who authorized worship and its use of psalms in Jerusalem."[1] It may be helpful for you to imagine these words being written by someone just like yourself who is experiencing both the challenges of life and the hope in God's abiding presence.

A few selected verses will then help you focus on a "theme word" to connect with the psalm more deeply. Finally, you will be invited to pause with a simple spiritual practice that you can take with you into the week as you explore new ways to nurture your life of faith during the Lenten season.

This invitation to pause with the Psalms begins with Ash Wednesday and focuses on Psalm 51 and the theme "A Clean Heart." The rest of the chapters pair psalms with the following themes: "Paths," "Faces," "Blessing," "Tables," "Waiting," "Thanksgiving," "Listening," "Being Alone or Abandoned," and "Hands." Each psalm and each theme invite you to engage with your head and your heart. This study invites you to step into a psalm—to use your brain to hear it in new ways, to encounter new scholarship, different translations, and paraphrases, but also to find space for renewal, refreshment, and prayer. Each chapter closes by inviting you to take up a spiritual practice such as a breath prayer, walking or moving along a path or labyrinth, or reviewing your day using a prayer called the Examen.

May this Lenten journey be a welcome interruption in the rhythms of your daily life. May you find the space and the time for just a few minutes each day to let God's Spirit awaken and renew your spirit.

Reflection for Ash Wednesday

Psalm 51: A Clean Heart

When I lived in Chicago, I loved to go downtown for a midday Ash Wednesday service at my church, Fourth Presbyterian. For a brief moment during the service, I would pause to take in all the crosses on foreheads around me—some sharply defined, some just a smudge, some slightly hidden by hair, some clearly visible. When they received their ashes, these cross-bearers may have heard the words "From dust you came and to dust you will return" or my favorite rendition, which comes from my friend Rev. Abby Mohaupt: "From topsoil we come, to topsoil we return, and always we belong to God."

As I walked out of the church, I saw the faces of people who had just left their own Ash Wednesday services and were headed back to work or home or other places and were wearing a sign of their faith. I joined the cross-marked pilgrims walking the sidewalks on Michigan Avenue, wanting to ask them the questions I wrestled with: What does this mean for you, this chalky black symbol you are wearing? How will the next forty days make a difference in your life of faith?

Attend to Psalm 51

The season of Lent in the Christian calendar begins with Ash Wednesday. Psalm 51 is often included in services on this day. As you read the psalm, pay attention to particular words, to the requests of the psalmist, and consider how this psalm connects you with the Lenten season as it prepares you spiritually to move with Jesus toward the events of Holy Week and Easter.

Psalm 51 (Common English Bible [CEB])

Prayer for Cleansing and Pardon

For the music leader. A psalm of David, when the prophet Nathan came to him just after he had been with Bathsheba.

¹Have mercy on me, God, according to your faithful love!
    Wipe away my wrongdoings according to your great
        compassion!
²Wash me completely clean of my guilt;
    purify me from my sin!
³Because I know my wrongdoings,
    my sin is always right in front of me.
⁴I've sinned against you—you alone.
    I've committed evil in your sight.
That's why you are justified when you render your verdict,
    completely correct when you issue your judgment.
⁵Yes, I was born in guilt, in sin,
    from the moment my mother conceived me.
⁶And yes, you want truth in the most hidden places;
    you teach me wisdom in the most secret space.

⁷Purify me with hyssop and I will be clean;
    wash me and I will be whiter than snow.
⁸Let me hear joy and celebration again;
    let the bones you crushed rejoice once more.
⁹Hide your face from my sins;
    wipe away all my guilty deeds!
¹⁰Create a clean heart for me, God;
    put a new, faithful spirit deep inside me!
¹¹Please don't throw me out of your presence;
    please don't take your holy spirit away from me.

¹²Return the joy of your salvation to me
   and sustain me with a willing spirit.
¹³Then I will teach wrongdoers your ways,
   and sinners will come back to you.

¹⁴Deliver me from violence, God, God of my salvation,
   so that my tongue can sing of your righteousness.
¹⁵Lord, open my lips,
   and my mouth will proclaim your praise.
¹⁶You don't want sacrifices.
   If I gave an entirely burned offering,
   you wouldn't be pleased.
¹⁷A broken spirit is my sacrifice, God.
   You won't despise a heart, God, that is broken and crushed.
¹⁸Do good things for Zion by your favor.
   Rebuild Jerusalem's walls.
¹⁹Then you will again want sacrifices of righteousness—
   entirely burned offerings and complete offerings.
   Then bulls will again be sacrificed on your altar.

The season of Lent invites us to look closely at our lives, our words, and our actions. Psalm 51 is read on Ash Wednesday as we prepare to undertake this examination for the next several weeks because it reveals the writer's deeply personal struggle with faithful living in response to God's mercy, compassion, and faithful love. This psalm has been described by biblical scholar Walter Brueggemann as a psalm of disorientation, one that describes a life that is in disorder and the desire of the writer to return to a new life with God. It is identified in the Bible as written by David. Biblical scholars do not think David directly wrote any of the psalms. Rather, they believe that as the book was being formed, editors assigned psalms to David to fit particular times in his life. Psalm 51 is a good example of that. Attributed to David in its title, this psalm invites the reader to peer into David's anguished soul and confident faith, even as it reveals the kind of self-examination and affirmation of faith that can also be our practice during Lent. To emphasize this personal connection and journey, I will sometimes refer to David as the writer of a psalm that has been attributed to him.

At the center of the psalm, the writer makes his request to God for "a clean heart." The dark mark of an Ash Wednesday cross stands in sharp contrast to the imagery of a heart that is clean and open to God's love, God's mercy, and God's compassion. When we receive the ashes, we are reminded of our humanness, the ways we mess up, the things we do that grieve God's heart, and our dependence on God's loving mercy. And then right in front of us in this psalm we find the opposite—a clean heart.

One way to connect with why the editors of the book of Psalms assigned this one to David is to remember the history of David's life. He had been on a path that was not leading to good outcomes (a bit of an understatement!). After seeing Bathsheba at a distance, claiming her for his own, and impregnating her, David sent her husband Uriah to the front lines of battle, assuring his death and clearing the way for David to marry Bathsheba without being found out. When God's prophet Nathan confronted him about his actions, David experienced deep distress and a crisis of conscience. This psalm provides us with a glimpse into the writer's soul as we read these words of confession of his sin and his affirmation of God's presence. Psalm 51 is one of seven psalms attributed to David that are described as penitential because of the way he expresses remorse for his sins.

As you read it, notice what the writer is saying, and consider how it connects with your life of faith. In verses 1–5, we hear a confession of sin and a request for God's mercy. The author understands his sin to be the things he has done that are wrong and that have caused his profound guilt, even to the extent of identifying his actions as being evil in the sight of God. Within this confession, the author also provides a glimpse of God, who will forgive his sin, who will "have mercy."

Verses 6–14 comprise the middle of the psalm, where the author makes his request of God for restoration. Notice the words he uses to describe what he knows to be true. He wants to be clean ("purify me," "wash me"). He wants to know joy and happiness again. He wants forgiveness ("hide your face," "wipe away"). Rather than feeling separated from God and God's spirit because of his sin, the writer wants to return to a time when he knew God's presence was with him.

Verse 10 forms the centerpiece of his request to God. The psalmist doesn't just want forgiveness. He doesn't just want God to turn away from his sins. This person wants to start over, moving on from the place of sorrow and distress in which he has been living. The only thing that will make that possible is for God to give him a clean heart. This clean heart the author desires is one that will be filled with God's "new, faithful spirit."

Throughout this book, we will be exploring different translations and paraphrases of selected verses from each of our psalms. You may have a favorite translation or a beloved Bible. Or maybe you don't know where to begin to make a choice about which translation to read. It's not unlike going to the grocery store to buy cereal and being overwhelmed by so many choices. Different translations offer us the chance to see how different biblical scholars interpret a text as they read it in the original language—in this case, Hebrew. Paraphrases are different in that the author doesn't rely on the original language but rather works to make the text understandable in a contemporary culture. Both help us to engage in seeing similarities and differences in the text and discovering how they speak to us. Pause for a few minutes with three translations and two paraphrases of verse 10:

> Create in me a clean heart, O God,
>> and put a new and right spirit within me.
> —*New Revised Standard Version Updated Edition*
>> (NRSVue)

> Create a clean heart for me, God;
>> put a new, faithful spirit deep inside me!
>> —CEB

> Create for me a pure heart, Holy One;
> renew in me a spirit of purposeful direction.
>> —Pamela Greenberg, *The Complete Psalms:*
>> *The Book of Prayer Songs in a New Translation*

> I need a new heart and a fresh surge of courage.
>> —*The Manhattan Psalter: The Lectio Divina*
>> *of Sister Juanita Colon* (paraphrase)

> God, make a fresh start in me,
>> shape a Genesis week from the chaos of my life.
>>> —Eugene Peterson, *The Message*
>>> (MSG) (paraphrase)

The first three translations from the Hebrew describe the author's petition to God as asking for a right or faithful spirit, or a renewal in him of a "spirit of purposeful direction." If we think about this psalm in relation to David's life, it makes us wonder about the recent changes he experienced and how his sinful actions were right in front of him, at the heart of his confession, stirring in him the desire for something very different. He must have remembered a time in his life when God's spirit was alive and well in him. It is that which he wants to be renewed.

The paraphrases of Psalm 51:10 provide additional perspectives. Here we see two interpreters describing the psalmist's request for a "fresh surge of courage" and a new beginning like "a Genesis week." Both describe David's desire for a chance to renew his relationship with God, one that would require living in fresh ways so that his spirit would embody the creative energy of God's spirit of mercy, compassion, and faithful love.

In verse 11, David asks for God's presence, God's spirit, to be with him. In addition to desiring his own spirit to be more faithful to God, he wants God's spirit to be present—to be near, accessible, alive in him.

This psalm concludes in verses 15–17 with a promise to praise God and a reaffirmation of what the author believes God desires. Verse 15 may be familiar to you, as it is often used as a response in worship: "Lord, open my lips, and my mouth will proclaim your praise." This psalm begins with a confession of sin, moves to a petition for forgiveness and a chance to begin again, and concludes with a promise of praise to God. These last verses reveal a much different spirit within the writer.

Confident in God's faithful love, mercy, and compassion, the writer is now able to praise God and proclaim with assurance the kind of spirit that God wants. It is described as "a broken spirit." It is interesting to consider what the writer means here. "Broken" often has negative connotations, but one possible interpretation is that this is describing a spirit that is broken open, ready to receive. Perhaps a

broken spirit is also one that is not perfectly formed, that is still growing, ready to attend to the kind of spirit God embodies. Maybe it is a
spirit that is a bit rough around the edges. Maybe, knowing that it is
imperfect, it is one that waits.

In reading this psalm, it's easy to hear the psalmist's singular voice
of penitence and petition to God. But it's important to remember
that the psalms were an expression of a worshiping community. The
hearers of this psalm in worship in the temple would have known
that the confession and offering of praise to God require a response,
both individual and communal. And we are left to wonder what kind
of communal responses the worshiping communities of Israel might
have offered.

Hearing this psalm at the beginning of Lent is an invitation for
each of us to consider our responses in gratitude for God's faithful
presence. What words and actions would give evidence of God's
indwelling spirit in your heart?

Connect with a Clean Heart

Receiving a cross on my forehead on Ash Wednesday is still a practice that helps me center my attention on beginning my journey
through Lent. I wear the smudged cross on my forehead all day
until I look in the mirror at night. Slowly I wash it off. And I look
and think. What paths will I take this Lenten season? What inten-
tions do I have for moving into this season with my whole heart,
however smudged it is? Is there a spiritual practice I'd like to begin?
Is there something to take up and continue for these five weeks,
something that speaks to my heart? How can I make space for
God's breath, God's spirit to fill my heart?

Eugene Peterson's paraphrase of Psalm 51:10—"shape a Genesis week from the chaos of my life"—provides a way for us to hear
this ancient psalm in new ways. Imagine the beginnings of this good
earth as told by the author of the creation story in Genesis 1:1–24a.
God's breath, God's spirit, God's wind blew, and the world came
alive, and it was all good.

I hear again the words that marked me this day: "From topsoil
we come, to topsoil we return, and always we belong to God." This

blessing uses the translation "topsoil" from Genesis 2:7 in the CEB, rather than that of "dust." It is a reminder that God created humans not from dry dust but from the richest, darkest, most fertile soil. Only the best for God's creation! And in this blessing is also the promise that in our entire life span—the living we do between our beginning and our last breath—always and ever we belong to God.

Recalling all those smudged faces I saw walking around, I wonder now about the difference those dark marks of soil made in individual lives. And I wonder, too, about the difference they made in the congregations where those persons received the ashes. And then how did those marks of ash move those communities of faith into actions of justice, mercy, and kindness in the world?

Pause with Your Heart Each Day

I was sharing lunch with a friend who is Muslim. While we were eating, her phone dinged with what I thought was a message. She told me she kept reminders of prayer times on her phone so that she would remember to stop and pray. After I asked if she wanted to attend to her prayer, she said she would pray after our meal together. I realized then how much I didn't know about her prayer tradition. I learned from her that Muslims pray five times a day: sunrise, noon, afternoon, sunset, and night. These prayers are called *salat*, and they can be said alone or with others. The intention of this practice of prayer over the course of a day is to help the faithful remember their connection with God.

What helps you remember your connection with God? Over the course of a day, do you ever pause with a simple prayer of praise or thanksgiving or confession or petition? I think sometimes Christians don't know how to pray, or they think prayers have to sound like the ones they hear in worship. Or perhaps many wonder about the efficacy of prayer—does it make a difference?

For me, prayer is a way of connecting my heart with God. It's an opening, a window to wonder, a pause within ordinary time to let the holy find room. Two simple practices of prayer during this season of Lent will help you remember and maybe discover again ways that you are connected with God's spirit.

A heart prayer is a simple way of connecting your spirit with God's life in you. Place your hand on your heart. Feel its beating. Notice the rhythm. Reflect on the words of this psalm and the images that are evoked for you as you read it. Consider the places in the psalm where you connect with the psalmist's words. This writer knows God to be merciful, loving, wise. Think about the ways you know God, the ways that you experience God's presence in your life. Pause as you notice both your breath and the beating of your heart.

A breath prayer is another simple spiritual practice that can be used with this psalm. This simple prayer form is one that invites you to say a prayer that can be repeated in one breath. There are two verses in this psalm that lend themselves to this kind of prayer: "Create a clean heart for me, God; put a new, faithful spirit deep inside me!" (v. 10) and "Lord, open my lips, and my mouth will proclaim your praise" (v. 15).

Try a breath prayer by breathing in while saying silently, "Create a clean heart for me, God." Then breathe out while saying, "Put a new, faithful spirit deep inside me." Or do the same with "Lord, open my lips, and my mouth will proclaim your praise."

Find a time and place today and each day in the beginning of Lent to pause. Perhaps it's before a meal, or on a walk, or as you wake with your water, tea, or coffee, or before you go to bed. Or just maybe you want to find more than one time a day! Let this breath prayer be on your lips. And when a day seems busy or when you notice a moment of God's loving-kindness, stop and simply put your hand on your heart and breathe. Open your heart to God's spirit dwelling within you. And remember that always you belong to God.

Questions for Reflection

1. How does the psalmist describe God's character in the opening verses?
2. What is the psalmist saying about himself? What is he asking God to be or do?
3. What confession is on your heart this Lenten season?
4. What would a clean heart look like for you?

First Week of Lent

Psalm 25: Paths

Sometimes the way forward is very clear. And sometimes you can barely see the path. When walking in a field, it's possible to follow those who've preceded you as you take steps in the grass bent down by their footsteps. Other times, you make the path. You're the first one to set out, and others will follow the path you have made.

I find interacting with young children as they grow and develop so revealing about how personalities and interests combine at an early age. I was twelve when my younger brother was born. It was clear from the way he manipulated toys that his brain worked differently from those of my other siblings. From an early age, he liked to build and design structures.

One of our favorite family stories is about the time when I was in high school and getting ready to go out with friends. We were all seated at the dinner table together, and I got up from the table a bit early to finish getting ready. I tried to open the door from the kitchen to the hall, and when I did, by opening it, the other set of doors from the hall to the kitchen closed in my face. There was no way out. I was beyond frustrated. And there sat my little brother, quietly smiling. Unknown to the rest of us, he had spent most of the day rigging string up and around so that when one door opened, the others closed. My path was blocked, and only he knew how to let me out. It's such a vivid memory. It was clear at an early age that he could be an architect or engineer. No such clarity about a path forward in life at such an early age was apparent for me or my other siblings, though we all eventually found the vocational paths that were right for us.

One of the yearnings we all share is to see clearly, to know what's ahead, to find our own way through life. But we also know that paths through life change. Sometimes the path feels blocked or uncertain. Sometimes the only constant is change itself. And following a path or paths requires adaptability and the ability to deal with change. Lent gives us a chance to pause in the midst of all this change and listen to the music and rhythm of our lives. It offers us time to reflect on our journeys, where we've been and where we might be headed.

This defined season—five weeks that begin with the liturgy of receiving a mark of dirt or ash on our foreheads, a symbol for the journey toward Holy Week and then Easter—is a familiar path for many of us. It provides us a chance to connect more deeply with the faith that nurtures and sustains our being and the witness of our lives as we engage in acts of justice, mercy, and kindness. As you read and pause with verses from Psalm 25 this week, consider the paths your faith has taken over the span of your life.

Attend to Psalm 25

You may hear Psalm 25:1–10 read on the first Sunday of Lent. Again attributed to David in its title, this psalm is written in the form of an acrostic, with each verse beginning with a different letter of the Hebrew alphabet. As you read, notice what the psalmist is asking for in this psalm of petition or expression of need.

Psalm 25 (NRSVue)

Prayer for Guidance and for Deliverance
Of David.

> ¹To you, O LORD, I lift up my soul.
> ²O my God, in you I trust;
>   do not let me be put to shame;
>   do not let my enemies exult over me.
> ³Do not let those who wait for you be put to shame;
>   let them be ashamed who are wantonly treacherous.

[4]Make me to know your ways, O LORD;
   teach me your paths.
[5]Lead me in your truth and teach me,
   for you are the God of my salvation;
   for you I wait all day long.

[6]Be mindful of your mercy, O LORD, and of your steadfast love,
   for they have been from of old.
[7]Do not remember the sins of my youth or my transgressions;
   according to your steadfast love remember me,
   for the sake of your goodness, O LORD!

[8]Good and upright is the LORD;
   therefore he instructs sinners in the way.
[9]He leads the humble in what is right
   and teaches the humble his way.
[10]All the paths of the LORD are steadfast love and faithfulness,
   for those who keep his covenant and his decrees.

[11]For your name's sake, O LORD,
   pardon my guilt, for it is great.
[12]Who are they who fear the LORD?
   He will teach them the way that they should choose.

[13]They will abide in prosperity,
   and their children shall possess the land.
[14]The friendship of the LORD is for those who fear him,
   and he makes his covenant known to them.
[15]My eyes are ever toward the LORD,
   for he will pluck my feet out of the net.

[16]Turn to me and be gracious to me,
   for I am lonely and afflicted.
[17]Relieve the troubles of my heart,
   and bring me out of my distress.
[18]Consider my affliction and my trouble,
   and forgive all my sins.

^{19}Consider how many are my foes
  and with what violent hatred they hate me.
^{20}O guard my life and deliver me;
  do not let me be put to shame, for I take refuge in you.
^{21}May integrity and uprightness preserve me,
  for I wait for you.

^{22}Redeem Israel, O God,
  out of all its troubles.

Psalm 25 has a simple form that includes the beginning (vv. 1–3), the large middle section of the psalmist's prayer to God (vv. 4–15), and the conclusion (vv. 16–21). In their commentary on this psalm, Walter Brueggemann and William H. Bellinger Jr. have noted five themes. First, the writer seems to be in a critical situation. He is concerned about his enemies and his sins, the things that cause him distress. He seems to be in a really difficult time in his life. Yet in the midst of these difficulties, notice how he describes his faith. He waits for God (vv. 3, 5, 21). This is not a passive waiting. This person is confident that in his waiting, God will not abandon him.

A second theme is hope. The psalmist affirms God's *hesed*— "steadfast love" (NRSVue), "faithful love" (CEB)—three times. In verses 6, 7, and 10, God's mercy and *hesed* are affirmed. The psalmist asks God to remember him with *hesed* and not his past sins and describes God's paths as ones of *hesed* and faithfulness for those who keep God's covenant. The third theme of God's faithfulness, exhibited in God's covenant relationship with humankind, is described intimately in verse 14 as God's "friendship." Within the frame of affirming who God is in this psalm, we also read the writer's confession of sin in verses 7, 8, 11 and 18. The fourth theme of confession acknowledges how he has failed and now seeks God's forgiveness.

The last theme in this psalm is evident in the way that the psalmist balances the failures or sins in his life with his faith in God's love, mercy, and forgiveness. While acknowledging his failures, he is also confident in God's abiding presence. In verses 15 and 16, the psalmist writes how "my eyes are ever toward the LORD, for he will pluck my feet out of the net. Turn to me and be gracious to me, for I am lonely and afflicted" (NRSVue). As another scholar has observed, "The poet desires to be freed from the narrow space, set in a large space (v. 17)."[1]

Bellinger and Brueggemann write that "this mismatch between human ambiguity and divine singularity is the hallmark of biblical faith."[2] Waiting for God, hoping in God's steadfast love, God's covenanting presence with humankind in spite of or maybe because of our failures—these become the marks of one who follows in the paths of God.

In several of these chapters you'll read verses translated from Hebrew by Robert Alter. If you look up the verses in *The Hebrew Bible*, you may notice that some of the verses have different numbers than those of other translations cited here. In English translations like the NRSVue and the CEB, superscriptions like "Of David" or "For David" are placed before the first verse of the psalm. Alter follows the tradition of Hebrew Bibles in beginning the psalm with the superscriptions as the first verse.

Spend some time with a few of these verses in different renderings (vv. 4, 8, and 9), noticing the variety in expression. These first three are translations from Hebrew:

> Your ways, O LORD, inform me,
>   Your paths, instruct me.
> . . . .

> Good and upright is the LORD.
>   Therefore He guides offenders on the way.
> He leads the lowly in justice
>   and teaches the lowly His way.
>   —Robert Alter, *The Hebrew Bible*, vol. 3,
>   *The Writings* (Ketuvim)

> Make your ways known to me, LORD;
>   teach me your paths.
> . . . .

The LORD is good and does the right thing;
     he teaches sinners which way they should go.
God guides the weak to justice,
     teaching them his way.
                                              —*CEB*

Your roads, God, let me know them.
Your pathways, help me recognize them from the rest.
. . . .

You are gentle and straightforward,
guiding those who stray on the path—

leading the humble to walk in justice,
teaching the willing the holy road.
               —Pamela Greenberg, *The Complete Psalms*

Show me how you work, GOD;
School me in your ways.
. . . .

GOD is fair and just;
He corrects the misdirected,
Sends them in the right direction.

He gives the rejects his hand,
And leads them step-by-step.
                    —*MSG* (paraphrase)

I'm struck by the differences in these versions of Psalm 25. Both the NRSVue and the CEB translate verse 4 in the same way, with David asking God to teach him, to make paths known or visible or available to him. Pamela Greenberg's translation has a less didactic tone, one that is more invitational. Her translation, both of verse 4 and the following verses, acknowledges what I think many people of faith wrestle with: there are so many choices along the path we call life. The ability to discern good paths from unhealthy paths,

paths that lead to acts of justice and kindness, the "holy road" as she describes it—that is what David is asking for in his petition to God.

And then there's the intriguing paraphrase by Eugene Peterson of verse 4—"Show me how you work, GOD; School me in your ways." This is very different from the NRSVue translation: "Make me to know your ways, O LORD; teach me your paths." Comparing these two invites us to consider our own relationship with God's activity in our lives and in the world. In the NRSVue, the psalmist asks for help in seeing the paths that God has made known. Peterson's paraphrase shifts this responsibility to God: "Show me how you work."

Also, compare the differences and similarities in verses 8–9. Note the ways God is described as one who guides, teaches, leads, corrects. The experiences of this psalmist invite our own considerations of God's presence with us as we follow the paths of our life.

Do you think that the paths of faith God was showing this person were there all along but he had failed to see the works of God, the visible expression of God's steadfast love and faithfulness? Could it be that God is the one who has been waiting on the psalmist?

Connect with Paths

The paths of faith that I inherited have continued with me throughout my life. Two memories remind me of the ways that spiritual formation was set out for me as a path, a way forward in life. When I was a child, my parents had the sabbath practice of going to church on Sunday and taking us to church school. They immersed us in a faith community in the same ways they had been. The other memory is of a much-loved Bible story book that I read at night before bed. It did not have many pictures, but the stories were told so vividly that I could see them in my mind.

Otherwise, the paths of faith that were modeled at home were more implicit than explicit. I think my sister and brothers and I learned as much from what our parents did—the witness of their lives—as we did at church. I'm glad we had both: a faith community that surrounded and supported us and promised to be a faithful partner in our faith formation, and faithful parents who loved us and taught us that everyone was equal in God's eyes. I am thankful that the God I learned about at church and at home was a loving God, much like God as described by the writer of this psalm. The paths of faith that I observed at home were like the ones described in this psalm. God wants all persons of faith to follow the paths of justice and loving-kindness that God makes visible before us.

How has your path of faith been enriched or hindered by the ways you have come to or continue to understand the nature of God's relationship with humankind? What are your earliest memories of how God was first described to you? Did you hear people talk about God as an unforgiving critic and judge? Or did you know God as a God of mercy and steadfast love as is written in Psalm 25?

To see a way forward sometimes requires vision, strength, and imagination. This psalmist is honest about the threats in his life and his guilt over the sins he has committed while also affirming his trust in God's presence and confidence that God will hear him. As you read this psalm you get a sense that the path his life has followed has not always been easy. He longs for a path wider than the narrow one he has followed, and he has confidence that God will be a refuge for him along the way.

Think about your life of faith and the paths you have taken. Would you like a do-over for some of those paths? Consider the people who have been most significant in your life of faith, whose paths have been a model for you. In the words of Pamela Greenberg, who has made the "holy road" visible to you? Sometimes the path ahead seems ambiguous and there are many options for a way forward. Consider specific acts of justice, mercy, and kindness that have been visible in the paths you have walked or in the paths others that you admire have followed.

Waiting for God and taking refuge in God are two of the ways the psalmist writes of God's spirit being present in his life. As you pause with the image of a path during this first week of the Lenten season, consider how you wait for God or have sought protection in God.

Pause with Your Heart Each Day

Walking a labyrinth is a very old spiritual practice of mobile contemplation and prayer. It's a form of active meditation. Labyrinths can be found on the floors in churches or in gardens. There are even small hand labyrinths made out of cloth or wood so that you can follow a path with your finger.

People of all ages are drawn to this spiritual practice that invites you to enter and walk a path until you reach the center. There you are invited to pause, to meditate, to pray, to focus your mind and heart, to find your own center.

This week, try walking with a labyrinth or just walking a familiar or new path outside. Or you can walk with your fingers, following a labyrinth shape printed on a piece of paper. You can also sit inside and simply focus your gaze on a window and take in the movement you see.

Each day, perhaps at the same time, begin with quietly shutting off all the noise in your mind, all the distractions. Take a deep breath. As you follow a path with your eyes, your fingers, your legs, notice what's around you. Tune your ears to the sounds you hear, and focus on the people and places that have contributed to your life of faith.

As you begin this season of Lent, think about the people for whom you would like to pray. Name them as you walk with your fingers or your legs or as you observe movement from your chair. Are there people you know who are searching for paths in life? Name them. You may know people who have abandoned the path of faith in which they were raised and are searching for another way to experience God's steadfast love. Name them.

Close your time each day this week with Psalm 25:4: "Make your ways known to me, Lord; teach me your paths" (CEB).

Questions for Reflection

1. What is this psalmist asking for from God?
2. Now that you've read this prayer for guidance and deliverance, what are your own prayers for leading or rescue? Write them down or speak them to God.
3. What would a friendship with God look like for you?
4. What guidance are you seeking from God as you follow a path during this Lenten season?

Second Week of Lent

Psalm 27: Faces

The years of the pandemic were wearying for everyone. Trying to communicate behind masks and longing to see family and friends face-to-face, we all experienced the human desire for community and a return to normal interactions and conversations. We learned to live with a new reality of communication, searching for connection as we focused on eyes and gestures at a distance.

I think about that challenging time in our culture as I remember one of the great joys I have as a clergyperson. It was something we all missed those years when worship was remote. When serving Communion, I like to look at a person's face and call them by name. Holding the cup at just the right level for a child, a person in a chair, or a tall adult, I look them in the eye and repeat the familiar words, "[*Name*], this is the cup of salvation; it is for you." This is a sacred moment for me of looking into the eyes of a human. I want this child of God to pause just for a moment with the bread and cup, to hear the words while staying in this liminal space. I really want to whisper in their ear, "Don't move too quickly. Wait. Linger while we share this moment of looking into each other's eyes and hearing again the words of Jesus."

A parent left a young child alone with his new baby sister and overheard him whisper to her, "Can you tell me what God looks like? I used to know, but I'm beginning to forget." I love his question and his reasoning behind it—indeed, his theology. I've often thought that the youngest and the oldest people we know are the nearest to the presence of God's spirit. Like Moses who asked to see God (Exod. 33:18), don't we all yearn for that concrete and physical assurance of the One whose presence is ineffable and mysterious? In that memorable story, God assured Moses that God would be near but that he would not be able to see God's face.

As we continue moving through this season of Lent, Psalm 27 offers us a chance to think about God's presence in a way that is very different from the Gospel accounts of Jesus. Artists picture Jesus' face, and we can imagine how he appeared to his disciples and followers as he moved closer and closer to Jerusalem. This is not so with God the Creator, whose face is unknown. It is in that mystery of the unknown that we are invited to engage with this psalm attributed to David.

Attend to Psalm 27

The NRSVue titles this psalm "Triumphant Song of Confidence." As you read it, think about the title you would give it. And consider the affirmations that the psalmist is making about God.

Psalm 27 (CEB)

Triumphant Song of Confidence
Of David.

> ¹The LORD is my light and my salvation.
>   Should I fear anyone?
> The LORD is a fortress protecting my life.
>   Should I be frightened of anything?
> ²When evildoers come at me trying to eat me up—
>   it's they, my foes and my enemies,
>   who stumble and fall!
> ³If an army camps against me,
>   my heart won't be afraid.

If war comes up against me,
   I will continue to trust in this:
⁴I have asked one thing from the LORD—
it's all I seek:
   to live in the LORD's house all the days of my life,
   seeing the LORD's beauty
   and constantly adoring his temple.
⁵Because he will shelter me in his own dwelling
   during troubling times;
   he will hide me in a secret place in his own tent;
      he will set me up high, safe on a rock.

⁶Now my head is higher than the enemies surrounding me,
   and I will offer sacrifices in God's tent—
      sacrifices with shouts of joy!
   I will sing and praise the LORD.

⁷LORD, listen to my voice when I cry out—
   have mercy on me and answer me!
⁸Come, my heart says, seek God's face.
   LORD, I do seek your face!
⁹Please don't hide it from me!
   Don't push your servant aside angrily—
      you have been my help!
   God who saves me,
      don't neglect me!
      Don't leave me all alone!
¹⁰Even if my father and mother left me all alone,
   the LORD would take me in.
¹¹LORD, teach me your way;
   because of my opponents, lead me on a good path.
¹²Don't give me over to the desires of my enemies,
   because false witnesses and violent accusers
   have taken their stand against me.
¹³But I have sure faith
   that I will experience the LORD's goodness
   in the land of the living!

[14]Hope in the LORD!
   Be strong! Let your heart take courage!
   Hope in the LORD!

This psalmist certainly expresses confidence in God's presence with him. But there is a lot more going on as he vividly describes experiences of opposition from others. Look at the structure of the psalm and the ways that structure opens up the meaning. In verses 1–6, the psalmist affirms trust and confidence in God. Notice the metaphors that are used to describe God: light, salvation, fortress. Because of this trust in God's abiding presence, there is no fear of enemies. Verses 4–6 describe a desire to live in God's house where God will provide shelter. The psalmist writes how he will sing praises to God in thanksgiving for God's sheltering him from his enemies.

In verses 7–10, the focus changes to the psalmist's petitions of God. This transition in voice as he prays to God for help can be heard clearly. Notice the petitions to God to listen to his voice and be merciful and respond. The psalmist asks to see God's face revealed to him, not hidden, and knows that God would not push him away.

Finally in verses 11–14, after revealing his fears and making his requests for help known to God, the psalmist concludes with three specific requests and a final affirmation of faith. He wants to be familiar with God's ways. With his urgent request for God to show him paths to take "because of my opponents," it makes you wonder what paths would have been forced on him by his enemies. This hymn of faith concludes with an affirmation of belief in God's goodness and acknowledges that the strength of heart is made possible by hope. Notice the instruction that is repeated to "hope in the LORD!"

Consider these translated and paraphrased versions of verses 8–9a, noting similarities and differences:

   Come, my heart says, seek God's face.
      LORD, I do seek your face!
   Please don't hide it from me!
      Don't push your servant aside angrily—
         you have been my help!
                                    —CEB

Of You, my heart said:
　"Seek My face."
　　Your face, LORD, I do seek.
Do not hide Your face from me,
　do not turn Your servant away in wrath.
You are my help.
　　—Robert Alter, *The Hebrew Bible*, vol. 3,
　　　　　　　　The Writings (Ketuvim)

My heart cried out to you, "Look at me!" I've heard your hidden prompting in the depths of my soul urging me to turn to you, and I have, truly I have. Don't be angry with me, don't turn away from me, please. You've always come to my aid in the past; don't fail me now.
　　—*The Manhattan Psalter: The Lectio Divina of Sister Juanita Colon*
　　　　　　　　(paraphrase)

　　Each of the translations from Hebrew present David's desire to seek God's face very similarly. It is interesting to contrast the tone of David's plea in verse 9 with the confidence in God he expresses at the beginning of the psalm. I wonder about that change. Sister Juanita Colon adds an especially pleading tone to David's voice. In her paraphrase, the psalmist seems so afraid of his enemies that he is desperate to remember how God has been present with him in the past so that the divine presence will continue *now*.
　　In making his request to see God's face, this person is indeed asking for assurance that God's presence will be with him. Recalling other places in Scripture where God's face has been mentioned, we begin to gather the deeper meaning of this phrase. In an appearance to Solomon after the temple was built, God promised that the sins of the people would be forgiven and their land would be healed if they prayed and sought God's face (2 Chr. 7:14). Seeking God's face is an act of faith—a visible action that reveals belief, a relationship with God, a commitment to following a good path as expressed here. God's face also appears in Numbers 6:24–26, a lovely benediction often said or sung in worship. It is described as a priestly blessing that God told Moses to use in blessing the Israelites: "The LORD

bless you and protect you. The LORD make his face shine on you and be gracious to you. The LORD lift up his face to you and grant you peace" (CEB). When God's face is hidden, God's presence is removed. When God's face is present, God's people are assured of receiving God's care and blessing.

Have you been thinking about the title you would give Psalm 27 as we reflect on what it is expressing? I'm not convinced that this is a psalm of triumphant confidence. I think it's more complicated than that. I think it's a great psalm for us to read during this Lenten season, as we consider our human limitations and how to live faithfully, exactly because of its movement between deep confidence in God's presence and the anxiety and fear of facing difficult situations, enemies, fear, and wondering whether God is present or not.

This psalmist wants assurance that God's face will be turned toward him, not away. Isn't that also the question of faith we live with? Is God's face close to me when I encounter disaster, fear, my own sinfulness? Maybe an appropriate title for this psalm could be "A Song of Hope."

Connect with Faces

During the pandemic when ministers were preaching into cameras in empty sanctuaries, some taped headshots of church members to the pews or chairs so that the spaces would look less empty. Pastors and musicians who were accustomed to encountering the faces of the faithful of all ages in front of them and around them every week were helped by seeing those photographs. In this way they could remember the community that gathered virtually, as together across time and space they prayed for healing and hope, for a world where all people would be safe.

Whose faces are in front of you this day? Do you look into the face of the stranger holding up a cardboard sign asking for help at the stoplight? Or do you immediately grab your phone to check it so that you won't have to see that person's face? I confess that I sometimes do the latter. Is there a face you haven't seen in a while, perhaps someone you want a conversation with just to catch up? Or maybe there's a hard conversation you'd like to have with someone about a matter that concerns you deeply. Who are the enemies whose faces you would just rather not see? How hard is it to see the face of the enemy through God's eyes?

Lindsay P. Armstrong notes how we might be uncomfortable with a Lenten discipline that holds "fear and faith, doubt and trust together." She suggests that as Christians, "we form communities where people are allowed and taught to talk honestly. In response to the culture's deep and pronounced needs for connectivity and authenticity, we offer safe space, even to people whose lives, views of the world, or clothing style may not match our own."[1]

I think this psalm is an invitation for us to join with the writer in wrestling with the tension between honest doubts and fears, and faith and trust. This is what it means to encounter each other's faces and, together, the face of God—to be real, to be vulnerable. And the church can and should be a safe space for real, vulnerable, face-to-face conversation about issues of faith—those that divide us and those that unite us. Congregations that engage in courageous conversations about race, differences in sexual orientation and gender identity, faith traditions other than our own, immigration and refugees—add your issues to the list—are providing a space for honest wrestling with our full humanity, which only brings us more fully into the knowledge and presence of God.

As I think about those photos of the church family spread out over a sanctuary, I think about whose faces are pictured and whose are not. Now that we are back together and able to see one another face-to-face, I wonder if there are faces that are still not welcome. David longed to see the face of God and knew that when God's face was present and not hidden, God would be leading him on a "good path." And God's face is most completely seen when we see and acknowledge the faces of all whom God loves.

So who are the faces God sees that we don't?

- The trans young adult who asks to have a blessing for their new name
- The autistic child who needs help finding space to be present in worship
- The widow or widower who grieves the loss of a beloved partner

- The teenager wrestling with anxiety and depression who finds it difficult to make friends
- The parents who struggle to make ends meet
- The one whose body is covered with tattoos
- The older adult who can no longer live independently

Pause with Your Heart Each Day

The Psalter is the earliest hymnbook of the Jewish and Christian faiths, and the poetry of its hymns expresses many of the same challenges, fears, and hopes we have today. Psalm 27 offers a fairly simple form that you can follow to write your own psalm, one that holds together the tension between fear and faith, doubt and trust. For your spiritual practice this week, try writing or illustrating your own psalm using the guide below. (If the idea of writing or illustrating your own psalm is a bit daunting, that's okay. Instead, use Psalm 27 for your meditational reading this week, perhaps reading just a couple of verses each day.)

Some of us love to use words for faith expression. Others enjoy visual expressions. And then there are some who enjoy mixing words and images together. For you who are interested in visual expression, get out your markers, crayons, water colors, paints, fabric, wood, collage materials, or yarn, and let your mind and soul connect with this psalm form.

Try writing or illustrating:

- Words, phrases, sentences, and images that describe your trust in God
- Words, phrases, symbols/images that describe the ways God protects you
- Your prayer of help to God: What fear do you want to name or illustrate? For what are you asking God?
- Words of praise to God that are on your lips: What images come to mind when you think of God's presence and protection? What does the face of God look like for you? When God sees your face, what does God see?

Psalm 27 has several different movements:

- Affirming trust
- Naming fears and petitions to God
- Specific requests to God
- Words of affirmation and praise

Try matching your writing, ideas, and/or images to each movement, creating your own psalm. Begin by arranging words or ideas under each of these movements. Then you can continue to expand on your writing, as in a journal entry, or bring the pieces of your illustration together however it feels right to you.

May this psalm of deep faith in the face of God's abiding presence surround you as you walk a good path and observe the faces of God's beloved people around you this week. And as you tune into God's presence and the presence of others, perhaps with the psalmist you can affirm, "But I have sure faith that I will experience the LORD's goodness in the land of the living!" (v. 13, CEB)

Questions for Reflection

1. What is your title for Psalm 27? Does "Triumphant Song of Confidence" still fit, or does something else seem more appropriate to you?
2. Have you ever wondered about what God's face looks like? When God's face is turned toward you, what does God see?
3. Where are you struggling with doubt? What are your fears?
4. As you think about this time in your life of faith, for what are you most grateful?
5. Whose are the faces God sees and loves that you don't see?

Third Week of Lent

Psalm 63: Blessing

Soon after I moved to Chicago I asked someone, "How are you?" The response I got was "I am blessed." I had never heard someone respond that way; usually the response was "Fine" or "Good" or "Couldn't be better" or "Not so good" or "Livin' the dream." Thinking back to that experience so long ago, I wish I had paused and asked, "How would you describe some of the ways you are blessed this day?"

As we have made the cultural move from communicating and connecting with family and friends with handwritten notes and cards to texts, emails, video chats, and social media, it's common to hear or see the phrase "Blessings on your day" as the conclusion to a text or even its entire contents. Along with *best*, *love*, and *peace*, the word *blessings* has become a common sign-off in emails, especially among friends.

I wonder about the intention or feeling behind *blessings* when it's used in this way. Does it carry more significance than just a familiar way to respond? Has it become a way to acknowledge faith or belief? When written, does it have any feeling or expression behind it? For example, you're reminded on social media of someone's birthday and you read the 10 "Happy birthday" greetings posted on their account. So you write, "Blessings on your day." After doing that, do you pause to think about that person and the blessing you are giving them or how this person has been a blessing in your life?

Since I live in the South now, having returned to Tennessee where I was born, I hear the familiar comment "Well, bless your heart"

37

when one does not know what else to say in response to what someone else has just said. It's like that reminder from parents to children, "If you can't say something nice, don't say anything at all." "Bless your heart" works!

In worship in August or September, we bless backpacks of children and teachers to honor the spaces of learning they will encounter in a new school year. At the end of a worship service, the pastor offers us a blessing before the benediction as we leave to return to our life and work as God's faithful witnesses. We are sent with a blessing. We eat at tables and we bless our food and give thanks to God for the friends who nurture our souls and the food that nourishes our bodies.

We have many different ways of understanding what blessing is, what it means to receive a blessing, and what it means to give a blessing. For example, the act of offering a blessing at a meal is a way of giving thanks to God, of acknowledging the gifts of all those who have brought food to our tables. People who say they are "blessed" are acknowledging the gift of God's presence in their life. Maybe you've had the experience of someone saying to you, "You are a blessing in my life," and you recognize what your conversation or presence with them has meant for both of you—it is an experience of grace and goodness. When we receive a blessing from the minister at the end of worship, we leave knowing that with the reception of these words we are sent out to remember that everywhere we go during the week there will be opportunities to bless others and to receive a blessing.

As we move through the Lenten season, reflecting on psalms and some of the themes they raise, Psalm 63:1–8 provides a way for us to think about blessing as it is used in this hymn of trust in God, and it invites us to consider the ways that we experience blessing in our lives.

Attend to Psalm 63

I am drawn to the season of Lent because it provides a space for meditation, for listening for God's presence. In between the reminder of our human frailty on Ash Wednesday and the renewal of life at Easter, we can pause to await some sort of blessing without perhaps knowing exactly what we are looking for.

Psalm 63:1–8 is included in the Revised Common Lectionary for reading during Week 3 of Lent. The whole psalm is included here so that you can see how it concludes. As you read it, notice the imagery the writer uses to describe his longing for God and why he places his trust in God.

Psalm 63 (NRSVue)

Comfort and Assurance in God's Presence
A Psalm of David, when he was in the Wilderness of Judah.

[1]O God, you are my God; I seek you;
   my soul thirsts for you;
my flesh faints for you,
   as in a dry and weary land where there is no water.
[2]So I have looked upon you in the sanctuary,
   beholding your power and glory.
[3]Because your steadfast love is better than life,
   my lips will praise you.
[4]So I will bless you as long as I live;
   I will lift up my hands and call on your name.

[5]My soul is satisfied as with a rich feast,
   and my mouth praises you with joyful lips
[6]when I think of you on my bed
   and meditate on you in the watches of the night,
[7]for you have been my help,
   and in the shadow of your wings I sing for joy.
[8]My soul clings to you;
   your right hand upholds me.

[9]But those who seek to destroy my life
   shall go down into the depths of the earth;
[10]they shall be given over to the power of the sword;
   they shall be prey for jackals.
[11]But the king shall rejoice in God;
   all who swear by him shall exult,
   for the mouths of liars will be stopped.

There are several things to pay attention to in this psalm. We don't really know which wilderness time is referenced here. Scholars think the psalmist speaks in David's voice, referring to when he was a young man running away from Saul. Notice how the wilderness setting connects you to David's physical and spiritual drought. And then he remembers the temple where he knew God's presence in a time when he wasn't hungry or thirsty but rather when he felt full of God's *hesed*—God's steadfast love.

The psalm follows a rather simple form. In verses 1–2, David's vivid words describe the depth of his longing for God. One commentary writer has suggested that "the psalm presents the ideas that longing is healthy, that thirst for God's presence invites and brings God's presence and that God's presence satisfies longings."[1] Think about this insight that longing is good. It is not representative of a lack but rather an indication of a strength, of insight and health.

Verses 3–5 offer the psalmist's words of praise and blessing. Verse 3 is the clearest statement of David's faith; he proclaims that the steadfast love of God is better than life. What is that saying about David? And more important, what is it saying about God? In his brief commentary on this psalm, J. Clinton McCann Jr. writes, "In a real sense, 'steadfast love' is something like a one-word summary of the character of God."[2] It's a familiar term used frequently in other psalms and in other settings to describe a person's experience of the constancy of God's love.

Verses 6–8 express the writer's confidence in God's abiding presence. Notice the psalmist's repetition of the word *soul* in verses 1, 5, and 8. His soul thirsts. It is satisfied. And in verse 8, the psalmist describes his soul as clinging to God. The image of David holding on to God as God's right hand reaches out to support him frames the words of David's trust in God's presence with him.

The reading of Psalm 63 during Lent ends with verse 8, but as you have read above, the psalm continues with three final verses that have a very different tone from the rest of the psalm. The writer moves quickly from faithful praise and trust in God's steadfast love to words of vengeance and a final statement of response. In his commentary on this psalm for use in worship during Lent, Richard C. Stern writes: "The complete psalm offers the more realistic ebb and flow of the appropriation of God's grace."[3] In other words, as human beings sometimes we are able to move with the Spirit of God, and other times we continue to reflect instincts of vengeance and violence, which are not of God.

Consider Psalm 63:2–4a and the differences you see in these translations and the paraphrase from *The Message.* As you read them, note the words or phrases that add to the translation at the beginning of this chapter or invite you to think about the ways you trust in God.

> So, in the sanctum I beheld You,
> seeing Your strength and Your glory.
> For Your kindness is better than life.
> My lips praise You.
> Thus I bless You while I live.
> —Robert Alter, *The Hebrew Bible*, vol. 3,
> *The Writings* (Ketuvim)

> Yes, I've seen you in the sanctuary;
> I've seen your power and glory.
> My lips praise you
> because your faithful love
> is better than life itself!
> So I will bless you as long as I'm alive.
> —CEB

> In holy places, I have gazed for you,
> hoping to witness your power and glory,
> for your kindness is better than life.

> My lips will praise you;
> I will bless you with my entire life.
> —Pamela Greenberg,
> *The Complete Psalms*

> So here I am in the place of worship, eyes open,
> drinking in your strength and glory.
> In your generous love I am really living at last!

My lips brim praises like fountains.
I bless you every time I take a breath.

—MSG (paraphrase)

Three ideas expressed in Psalm 63 and captured slightly differently in these translations and paraphrase catch my eye. First, the writer clearly knows God's presence when he is in the place of worship, the sanctum, the sanctuary, and holy places. But his awareness of God's presence is not confined only to the temple. In verse 6, he acknowledges how he feels close to God at night before bed. I wonder if this is the experience of faithful Christians today—that the experience of God's presence is named and known outside of holy places.

Second, notice the focus on blessing. In verse 4, the psalmist promises to bless God "while I live," "as long as I am alive," "with my entire life," "every time I take a breath." Wouldn't it be interesting to be able to ask the psalmist, "What do you mean when you say you bless God?" We all do it differently, I think. And we can do it as often as we breathe in and we breathe out, something those of us with healthy lungs take for granted.

Recall the activity of a breath prayer that was described on page 15. Breathe in with the air that fills your lungs, and breathe out with a blessing to God. In this breath, acknowledge that we bless God when we act faithfully in our interactions with others. We bless God when we work for justice. We bless God when we take care of all creation.

The translation by Pamela Greenberg offers a slightly different way of thinking about blessing God over the course of a lifetime: "I will bless you with my entire life." This promise seems to offer the comfort of knowing that though there are times when we feel absent from God's presence or estranged because of something we have done, God is there waiting, always present, renewing our connection over the course of our lives. We really can't mess it up.

The appropriateness of this psalm for our reading during Lent becomes clear. It invites our consideration of the ways that God sustains our life. The psalmist offers us a window into hearing how God's presence is experienced as a blessing in all phases of life. And in this opening of that window, we are invited to respond with the same honesty about our relationship with God, our own experiences of blessing and being blessed.

Connect with Blessing

The context for the speaker's praise and trust in God is worship in the temple. It is there where the psalmist experiences God's presence. Read the psalm again out loud. Notice how the psalmist describes a yearning for God's presence—as dry, as weary, as a land where there is no water. Have you ever been in that kind of parched place in your life of faith? What words would you use to describe it? Are they similar to or different from those of the psalm writer?

Confident in God's love, the psalmist moves to a bold assurance of God's presence. Eugene Peterson paraphrases Psalm 63:4 this way: "I bless you every time I take a breath." Often we think about how blessed we are. How often do we consider how the action of blessing is not one of receiving but rather one of giving? And in this psalm, the act of blessing is directed to God. These translators and interpreters have suggested we bless God with our whole lives, with every breath we take. We bless God while we live.

Sometimes in worship, prayers of confession are introduced as illustrating the ways we grieve God's heart with our failures. Imagine for just a moment how your recent words and actions bless God's heart, how they make God feel good and thankful that God's presence is always abiding with creation. Pause with this just for a moment.

This psalm offers us a window into the soul of one who knows God's intimate presence, one whose soul is blessed because of that relationship. This psalm can also be a model for our lives of faith. When we experience the blessings of God, we can and should look for the places and people with whom we can share something of the goodness, kindness, mercy, and love of God—to extend that blessing in turn. The blessing we know and experience can be shared.

Pause with Your Heart Each Day

Psalm 63:1–8 is rich with imagery as it expresses the speaker's trust in God. Try reading it each day this week either as you wake and start your day with a cup of tea, coffee, or water or before you close your eyes for restful sleep.

You could also try reading it using the ancient spiritual practice of *lectio divina*. In this contemplative way of reading, a passage is read three times. You can either read it yourself or listen to it read online. (One version I like can be found by searching for "Psalm 63 English Audio Bible AFCM.") Or consider inviting a friend or family member to join you this week in meditating on this psalm together. You can take turns reading it to each other as you engage with the practice of *lectio divina*. Here are the steps:

1. The first time you hear the psalm read, listen for a word that pops out for you, that draws your attention. Pause and think about the word, or share the word if you are doing this with someone else.
2. As you read or hear the psalm read a second time, think about an image that comes to mind. Share that image with the other person.
3. For the third hearing or reading of the psalm, consider how God is speaking to you in these verses. What is God's invitation to you this season of Lent?

Questions for Reflection

1. In what ways do you connect with the words or expressions of the psalmist describing the experience of trusting in God?
2. What are some places or times when you have experienced God's presence? What are some times in your life when you have longed for God's voice or presence?
3. As you reflect on your life experiences, what are some ways that you have blessed God, or what are some ways God has blessed your life?
4. God's presence can be experienced in our daily activities. God's presence is also known to us in the ways that friends, families, and even strangers bless our lives. When have you experienced this kind of presence or blessing?

Fourth Week of Lent

Psalm 23: Tables

When my grandmother moved out of her house and into a retirement apartment, she sent me her dining room tables and chairs. She loved collecting lovely furniture, and I was delighted to receive this gift. There were two tables. Each opened up, and when both were swiveled out together, twelve people could easily sit around them. The dining tables were rarely used, however, since my grandmother really didn't like to cook or entertain. Our Sunday evening family meals were always around a glass-top wrought-iron table in the breakfast room of her house.

I loved having these tables and chairs, because they provided room for more people to gather with me for a meal. Thanksgiving with family who drove to Chicago to spend the weekend with me and Easter brunch with neighbors and friends after early morning worship are two of my favorite memories of table gatherings.

When I moved to Nashville to join my husband in our condo, I knew the dining room would be too small for my grandmother's furniture. So my sister and I swapped. I got the table and chairs she had inherited from our great aunt, and she took our grandmother's furniture. Both tables carry memories for us of birthday celebrations, of holding hands as we sang our family blessing, and of the faces of all those whose stories we heard as we shared meals together.

Thinking about how the psalmist describes God's preparation of a table before him in Psalm 23 provides a good place for pausing during this week of Lent. If you grew up in the church and remember only one psalm, it's probably this one. You may have memorized it in the King James Version. That was a requirement of my confirmation class. It's still there in my memory bank.

There are so many images in Psalm 23. Perhaps you have a favorite. This beloved psalm is often read by congregations at Communion. Have you ever wondered why this expression of David's affirmation about God's presence with him like a shepherd is the psalm selected for reciting at the table where bread is broken and the cup is shared?

Once when I was leading a Communion service at a conference, I invited everyone to say or read Psalm 23 together. It was probably printed in the NRSV translation. When I began leading this psalm, I knew that the translation I had memorized when I was twelve would be the words I would say. I stood in front of this very large group and slowly stopped repeating it as I watched and listened to the congregation as they carried this beloved psalm with the beauty of their collected voices. There is just something about a community gathered, sharing words and the meal at the table, that can make our hearts sing. Thinking about this psalm during Lent provides us with the opportunity to consider some new meanings as we make the journey through this season of faith.

Attend to Psalm 23

Whether Psalm 23 is very familiar to you or whether you are reading it for the first time, there is much to notice. It may be the only psalm that is read in worship multiple times during the three-year Revised Common Lectionary cycle. You can hear it read during the season of Lent, after Easter, and after Pentecost. For those for whom it is very familiar, the challenge is to notice how ancient words and beautiful poetry can continue to comfort and challenge our lives of faith.

Psalm 23 (NRSVue)

The Divine Shepherd
A Psalm of David.

> [1]The LORD is my shepherd; I shall not want.
>   [2]He makes me lie down in green pastures;
> he leads me beside still waters;
>   [3]he restores my soul
> He leads me in right paths
>   for his name's sake.
>
> [4]Even though I walk through the darkest valley,
>   I fear no evil,
> for you are with me;
>   your rod and your staff,
>   they comfort me.
>
> [5]You prepare a table before me
>   in the presence of my enemies;
> you anoint my head with oil;
>   my cup overflows.
> [6]Surely goodness and mercy shall follow me
>   all the days of my life,
> and I shall dwell in the house of the LORD
>   my whole life long.

There are some interesting things to know about Psalm 23. It consists of fifty-five words in Hebrew, which means that the center of the psalm is the twenty-eighth word, "you"—"you are with me." The psalm is framed by the two references to God as Lord at the beginning and the end. The original audience hearing or singing this psalm would have understood "shepherd" as referencing a king, one who would watch over or protect those who lived in the realm where the king ruled.

Notice the shift in imagery as the psalm makes some literary moves. Verses 1–3 picture God's shepherding role—tending, leading, and feeding. In verse 3, the writer affirms that God "restores [his] soul." In his translation of this verse, Robert Alter notes that the Hebrew word *nefesh* does not mean "soul" but "life" or "life breath." And so he translates verse 3 "My life He brings back." He explains his choice: "The image is of someone who has almost stopped breathing and is revived, brought back to life."[1]

Perhaps one reason the psalm is so familiar and so beloved is that it affirms God's sustaining and shepherding presence. Pay close attention to verse 4, which adds another dimension. The Hebrew word *tsalmaveth*, which appears in the NRSVue as "the darkest valley," can also be translated "total darkness."[2] The psalm writer confesses that even when the path that is followed is not a desirable one, God is present. Verse 5 goes on to imagine God offering hospitality at a table. The psalm concludes with the simple faith statement of one who is assured of being in God's presence.

Pause with the first part of verse 6: "Surely goodness and mercy shall follow me." Walter Brueggemann and William H. Bellinger Jr. suggest that the psalmist "thought he was being pursued by dangers and threats, but in fact it was the providential goodness of God that was what had been following him and chasing after him. The alternative life made possible by such divine pursuit concerns the generous God of creation (goodness) and the faithful God of covenant (fidelity), who has been the subject's companion all along the way."[3] It is really a different concept of God's presence here. Rather than us seeking God's goodness and mercy, the psalmist reverses things. God's goodness and mercy find us.

Consider these recent translations and a paraphrase of Psalm 23:5 from *The Message*. In what ways do they invite your reflection on the table God sets before us?

> You set out a table before me
>   in the face of my foes.
> You moisten my head with oil,
>   my cup overflows.
> —Robert Alter, *The Hebrew Bible*,
>   vol. 3, *The Writings* (Ketuvim)

You spread a table before me
   in face of my greatest fears.
      —Pamela Greenberg,
      The Complete Psalms (v. 5a)

You set a table for me
   right in front of my enemies.
You bathe my head in oil;
   my cup is so full it spills over!
      —CEB

You serve me a six-course dinner
   right in front of my enemies.
You revive my drooping head;
   my cup brims with blessing.
      —MSG (paraphrase)

These translations appear fairly similar in describing who else is at the table—"in the face of my foes" or "right in front of my enemies." I wonder why the psalmist would express this act of God's hospitality in this way—setting a table where you have to face your enemies. I think about this verse when I take Communion and look at others who are coming to the table. Is everyone there my friend? Is there someone coming to the table I would consider to be my enemy—someone who has a different theology or a different political expression from me?

Looking closely at two translations opens this linguistic expression a bit more. Alter writes, "You set out a table before me in the face of my foes." And Greenberg translates it this way: "You spread a table before me in face of my greatest fears." Enemies or foes can be other people. God invites us to sit with them. Read together, Alter and Greenberg are suggesting that God invites us to sit at table with those people or things of which we are most afraid—whether external or internal. Either way, blessing with oil follows, as well as the confidence in God's abiding goodness and merciful presence.

In this fourth week of Lent as you pause with this psalm of trust, think about the tables set before you. Perhaps it's the Communion table at church where you are invited to sit and remember the words of Jesus about breaking bread and sharing the cup. A contemporary Communion hymn invites people to come to the table of grace, love, peace, and joy with the reminder that "this is God's table; it's not yours or mine."[4] Maybe it's a table you set in your own home or a table to which you are invited to share a meal. Recall tables from your childhood. This psalm concludes with the affirmation that God's goodness and mercy will always be present as a place is found in God's house. What kind of table might be in God's dwelling?

Connect with Tables

This familiar psalm is repeated together at Communion, read at the bedsides of those who are breathing their last breaths, and read again at their memorial service. It is taught at confirmation and embedded in our memories. It is poetry, eight simple yet complex verses. That's all it is.

Look at the middle of the psalm, "you are with me," and move out from there. If that's the center of the fifty-five Hebrew words, then perhaps it's where the writer wanted the hearer to focus. The phrase invites you to wonder what provoked this personal confession. Perhaps speaking in the voice of David, this writer knows God's presence in God's leading, restoring, comforting, preparing, and anointing actions.

Psalm 23 invites the reader to engage with three questions: What's the promise? What's the invitation? What's the challenge? Reread the psalm in light of these questions, and consider your response.

I think one promise is found right there in the middle of the psalm— that promise of God's presence, God's protection, God's guidance. The psalmist wrote the first two verses with the memory of a story passed down through generations of a God who always provided, a God whose presence was always there. Each day as you awaken, be aware of the ways God is present in your life. As you begin your day, remember those you know who are in need of God's presence, those people for whom you are praying, those people whom you are tending. Think about the rest of your week. With whom will you be sharing a meal, or a cup of tea or coffee at a table? In what ways is your presence comforting to another or comforting to you?

An invitation I see is found in verse 2, God's leading the poet to restful waters. It is an invitation then and now to slow down, to pause to rest body and soul. One of my favorite books for children about mindfulness or meditation is *Sitting Still like a Frog* by Eline Snel. One chapter is titled "The Conveyor Belt of Worries." Often we find it hard to be in God's presence when our mind and bodies are tight with worry, anxiety, or fear. This psalm reminds us to find the "still waters" that restore our souls.

Slowing down and pausing for refreshment, as though beside the still waters, can also be an invitation to be present with others who need our care. Sharing meals at tables with loved ones in retirement communities or health-care centers requires slowing down, getting into the rhythm that can indeed restore souls. Many congregations open their churches to feeding programs or places of shelter for the homeless—also a wonderful opportunity to slow down and accept the invitation to be present with those in need of food or shelter. Tables shared with strangers and guests remind us of the many places God invites us to go with the assurance we are never alone.

Finally, Psalm 23 offers a challenge—the challenge of facing enemies, foes, or even fears at the table, the table where God is also present. Coming to a table that includes diverse religious groups is one simple way to begin. In Charleston, South Carolina, Spirited Brunch happens once a year. Churches and religious communities open their doors and offer tables of food representative of their communities, giving them opportunities to socialize with diverse groups that may have been considered enemies at one time in religious history. In writing about this in her blog, *Edible Theology*, Kendall Vanderslice describes how at this brunch she will eat foods from Greek Orthodox, West African, and Latin American congregations, as well as Baptist and Episcopal churches: "We will taste the hospitality of Hindu, Jewish, Sikh and Bahá'í communities; we will enter the doors of Mother Emanuel AME—a community still so committed to hospitality that they will open their doors to hundreds of strangers on this day."[5]

With many cultural, religious, and political divides growing more deeply every year, I wonder if there's any way that sitting at table with those with whom we disagree, or even don't like, might be a way forward toward dialogue. It's one thing to sit at table with people who are different from us. It's quite another to sit down with those we really don't like, people with whom we really disagree, people who don't have the same values or hold the same political opinions we do. And sometimes we sit at table with family with all those differences represented, and, as Greenberg suggests in her translation, we face our fears. Then maybe we remember the center of the psalm, the affirmation that God is always present, restoring souls. Who would be on God's guest list at your table?

Pause with Your Heart Each Day

The Examen, a way of reviewing the day, is a very old spiritual practice of Ignatius of Loyola. It has a few simple steps. Some use this as a way to wind down at the end of the day. It's a practice that connects us to the heart of Psalm 23, God's presence with us, like gathering at the table in the quiet of the evening to talk about our day together. The Examen provides a way to review your day by reflecting on consolations—the good things that you experienced—and desolations—the things that troubled you or made you sad. Another way to approach the Examen is to think about thorns, roses, and buds. These images work wonderfully with children and teenagers or equally well with adults of all ages. Roses represent the good things that happened today; thorns are the tough things that happened or the things that made you sad; buds are things you are looking forward to.

During this fourth week of Lent, try pausing with the Examen each evening. You can try this alone or with a friend or family member. If it helps you to enter this practice with others, you could also have a FaceTime call or a Zoom gathering.

1. Settle into a comfortable spot and come into God's presence with silence or perhaps a simple affirmation: "God, I'm here; it's me." Some also find it helpful to light a candle or use a battery-operated votive candle during the Examen.
2. Recall the day silently for a few minutes, or if you are doing the Examen with children, name the events of the day.

3. Review the day more deeply: consolations and desolations. Where did you see or experience a sense of God's love today? Where did you notice God's presence? "I knew God was with me today when . . ." Where or when did you not feel the presence of God as closely as you wanted? Recall the places or moments you would like to revisit or do over. Ask for God's grace and healing as you reflect on those moments.
4. Look ahead to the next day and the opportunities it may offer you to experience God's presence in your life. Express your hopes for the day to God. In what ways can you share God's light and love with another?

Questions for Reflection

1. Which part of this psalm speaks to you? When has this psalm been a comfort for you?
2. The psalmist writes, "The LORD is my shepherd." How would you complete this sentence, "The Lord is my . . ."?
3. What stories from your experiences at tables help to connect you with Psalm 23?
4. What promise do you see in Psalm 23? What is the challenge? What is the invitation for you?

Fifth Week of Lent

Psalm 130: Waiting

Waiting is hard for me. I absolutely hate to waste time. I hate standing in lines. I'm an impatient waiter. Or maybe I'm just impatient in general. My challenge with waiting was put to the test years ago when my mother fell and broke her wrist. The day after that happened a major storm with straight-line winds knocked out the power grid in Memphis where she lived by herself in our family home. It was July. It was hot—very hot. My brother called from Pennsylvania to tell me what had happened. When I got there from Chicago, Mimi was sitting in the dark, in the heat, with her beloved dog, Butch, the one that she had rescued and that had just pulled her down on one of their first walks.

My family responded immediately with help. My cousin brought over a charcoal grill and a cooler with ice. My brothers checked in with phone calls. My sister sent her husband and teenage son with a generator, and they taught me how to use it, explaining how we could plug in only three things. My nephew showed me how to add gas, warning me of all the safety precautions and reminding me that I'd have to make sure I had enough gas each day to keep it running. My mother wanted to keep the freezer going, where she had frozen fresh vegetables from her garden. I wanted a coffee pot and air-conditioning. The former was possible; the latter was only a dream.

The first time I fell apart during this experience was at the store where I went to buy a fan and found they were sold out. A salesperson found me crying outside the store in 95-degree heat with 100-percent humidity and told me about another store that had fans in stock. I bought the biggest box fan I could find and plugged it in. And so the waiting began. Every day I would walk Butch around the neighborhood and look for power company trucks, phone trucks, anything that would signal that repairs were happening. And every day for ten days I saw nothing.

Daily trips to the gas station to keep the generator going provided opportunities to charge my cell phone so that I could talk with family and friends. We waited together—my mother, Butch, and I. In addition to the box fan, I bought novels for us to read, flashlights, and dog treats—something to help each of us survive the waiting.

Soon after I got there I offered to help my mother with a bath. I lit a candle and eased her into the tub. By the light of the candle, I gently washed her back. And I realized that I was now in a different time. It simply wasn't *chronos* anymore, ordinary clock time. It was *kairos*, or sacred time. I called it "Mimi time."

The busy, structured, and well-planned life I had left in Chicago was paused. And I realized that the only way to survive a situation over which I had no control was to find a way to accept that which was most difficult for me—waiting. Waiting in line for the gas that was rationed; waiting in line to get a bacon biscuit for Mimi for breakfast; waiting at the laundromat to wash our clothes; walking and waiting and praying for power to return. Wherever I went those weeks, I had a conversation with someone whose situation was more critical than ours—such as the mother trying to keep milk cold for her baby. We waited together.

Like the writer of Psalm 130, I knew what it was like to have my whole being hoping and waiting—hoping for healing for Mimi's broken wrist, hoping for an end to the power outage, and, with my whole being, waiting for a return to life as it had been for all who were impacted by that terrible storm.

In this fifth week of Lent, as you reflect on Psalm 130, find some moments to think about your own experiences of waiting, perhaps waiting with your whole being.

Attend to Psalm 130

Imagine for a moment that you are in a crowd of ancient pilgrims heading toward Jerusalem, climbing the hill to celebrate a religious festival like Sukkot (Feast of Booths), which commemorates Israel's time in the wilderness following the exodus and to mark the fall harvest. Psalm 130 would be one of the songs you would sing as you made your way closer to the wonderful celebration that awaited your arrival. This psalm is one of fifteen "Songs of Ascent" found in the latter part of the book of Psalms. They were called Songs of Ascent because of their references to Jerusalem and Zion. Jerusalem sits on a hill, so pilgrims on their way would repeat these shorter psalms from memory or sing them.[1] They include a variety of types of psalms reflecting the diversity of pilgrim voices—individual and communal laments, hymns of thanksgiving, wisdom psalms, and royal psalms focusing on the king.

When reading Psalm 130, we hear a singular voice expressing her lament to God. Read Psalm 130 in your Bible or the translation that is provided here. As you read, notice the lament the psalmist is expressing. What insights do you get about this psalmist's relationship with God?

Psalm 130 (CEB)

A pilgrimage song.
> [1]I cry out to you from the depths, LORD—
> [2]my Lord, listen to my voice!
>> Let your ears pay close attention to my request for mercy!
> [3]If you kept track of sins, LORD—
>> my Lord, who would stand a chance?
> [4]But forgiveness is with you—
>> that's why you are honored.

> [5]I hope, LORD.
> My whole being hopes,
>> and I wait for God's promise.

⁶My whole being waits for my Lord—
    more than the night watch waits for morning;
    yes, more than the night watch waits for morning!

⁷Israel, wait for the LORD!
    Because faithful love is with the LORD;
    because great redemption is with our God!
⁸He is the one who will redeem Israel
    from all its sin.

The psalm follows a fairly simple structure. Verses 1–2 offer the words of petition to God. Verses 3–4 acknowledge "sins." The NRSVue translates this word as "iniquities." In her commentary on this psalm, biblical scholar Nancy deClaissé-Walford notes that the word "iniquities" (*'avonoth*) is used two hundred times in the Old Testament to describe the sin of humans. The root meaning of the word is "to bend, curve, turn aside, or twist," thus providing a concrete image for a definition of "iniquity" as "an act, or mistake, which is not right or unjust."[2] Verses 5–6 describe expectant hoping and waiting. The last verses, 7–8, broadcast the words of the psalmist and the reminder of God's faithful love to the larger community.

See how three translations and *The Message*'s paraphrase of verses 5–6 provide a richness of engagement with this penitential psalm. Pause with each one, noticing what is similar and what is different.

I look for you, my soul looks for you wildly,
I wait for your word of response.

My soul longs for you
more than the watchman at the gate longs for morning,

more than the tired watchman at the gate
longs for the first flicker of dawn.
                    —Pamela Greenberg, *The Complete Psalms*

I wait for the LORD; my soul waits,
    and in his word I hope;
my soul waits for the Lord

more than those who watch for the morning,
more than those who watch for the morning.
—NRSVue

I hope, LORD.
My whole being hopes,
and I wait for God's promise.
My whole being waits for my Lord—
more than the night watch waits for morning;
yes, more than the night watch waits for morning!
—CEB

I pray to GOD—my life a prayer—
and wait for what he'll say and do.
My life's on the line before God, my Lord,
waiting and watching till morning,
waiting and watching till morning.
—MSG (paraphrase)

I wait and wait, my soul throbs with expectation. I'm like a watcher
scanning the horizon for the first light of dawn; no, more intent,
more eager.
—*The Manhattan Psalter: The Lectio Divina of Sister Juanita Colon*
(paraphrase)

Notice the different ways these versions describe the waiting—
waiting for God's response, waiting for God's promise, waiting to see
what God will say and do, waiting in God's word. Each indicates a
faithful and expectant kind of waiting in the assurance that God will
respond.

The psalmist compares the feeling of waiting for God with the
sentinels who stood guard on the third watch, waiting for the light
of day and breathing much easier when they knew they had made
it safely through another night. The poetic repetition of this phrase
adds emphasis and urgency to the experience of this one who waits.

In verse 7, the voice of the individual who has been heard in the
psalm calls on those who are also making the pilgrimage to "wait for

the LORD" (CEB). The Hebrew word is *yachal,* and when used here it invites the pilgrims not only to wait but also to hope, to expect something to happen. That single voice reminds the faithful pilgrims to wait and hope as they make their way to Jerusalem together. They move closer to Jerusalem, their voices now joined together, confident of the redeeming presence of God with them, the God who always also waits for them.

Psalm 130 is one of seven penitential psalms included in the Psalter. It has been used in liturgies during Lent since the medieval era. This psalm, sung by ancient pilgrims on their way to Jerusalem and by modern-day pilgrims making their way in this world, reminds us of the ways our words and actions (wrongdoings, sins, the record of our guilt) separate us from God.

In this last week of Lent, before we turn to the week called holy, we can join with pilgrims on their way to Jerusalem and consider the ways our words and actions have contributed to bending, turning aside, or twisting what we know to be right, while also declaring our longing and confidence as we wait for God's steady love to meet us on the path. Nancy deClaissé-Walford suggests that this psalm is an invitation to God's faithful people, "who embrace God's steadfast love, to help turn the tide of our world's and our own selfish iniquity—our self-seeking turning and twisting."[3] For pilgrims on their way to Jerusalem and for us today, we wait and hope, believing that "God, indeed, can redeem us from all of our 'iniquities'—our twisted ideas of what is right and wrong, of what is just and unjust."[4]

In spite of our bending, twisting, and turning aside, with the psalmist we give thanks for God's forgiveness and redeeming love. In her translation of this psalm, Pamela Greenberg describes God's presence as a "storehouse of kindness."[5] Thankfully, God's abundant love and patient waiting on our turning back to the holy path is a promise we can claim.

Connect with Waiting

Waiting to start my garden every spring is so difficult. The first warm days in early March call to me. But I know I have to wait. My neighbor and I share a mound at the front of her flower bed. I say "share" since she lets me plant it with her. Last year I planted zinnia seeds from packets I had bought. When my neighbor saw me outside, she gave me a bag of her own zinnia seeds that she had collected from the previous summer's garden. Now I save seeds like she does. I also browse through gardening catalogs to find zinnia seeds that are different from the previous year's collection.

Starting seeds indoors has become my Lenten practice, since I begin thinking about the garden as Lent begins. Then when it's warm enough, the soil is ready, and there's no danger of frost, I can plant the seeds and wait for them to sprout. This is a kind of waiting that I enjoy. I think of it as a gift from my mother. Mimi loved gardening, loved starting seeds in pots in the den and then moving them outside into the large brick planters my father had built for her on the patio. I think gardening nurtured her soul and connected her to the Creator, and she passed that spiritual practice to me.

Even as I confess my impatience and my dislike of waiting in the midst of discomfort, I realize that gardening also requires patient waiting. Seeds will sprout when they are ready. They can't be rushed. Plants will grow when they are given good soil and the right amount of light and water, and then the important role of the gardener begins, just as Eugene Peterson has paraphrased in *The Message*, the work of "waiting and watching ... waiting and watching." Sister Juanita Colon describes my experience: "I wait and wait, my soul throbs with expectation."

Waiting is hard. It's not a prized value in our culture. But as this psalm writer reminds us, waiting is an act of hope, a way of being present with expectant anticipation of God's redemptive and immanent life, always with us and waiting to emerge again and again.

Pause with Your Heart Each Day

As we move closer to the end of the season of Lent, let this practice of watching and waiting for life to return nurture your soul. Maybe you are a gardener like me and enjoy planting seeds and watching them grow. If not, give it a try. Find a packet of seeds at your local nursery or hardware store, and plant them in small pot. Place the pot near a window, water the seeds gently, and watch and wait.

Invite a family from church or the neighborhood to join you in planting seeds together. If visiting older adults at home or in assisted-living facilities is something you enjoy, plant some seeds in pots and take them with you on a visit. Watch them grow over time as you visit with your friend and care for the seeds together. If planting seeds is totally outside your skill set, then get help from a friend or buy a small houseplant. Or buy a pot with an herb like basil or parsley at the grocery store. Just give it some water, watch it grow, and use it in your cooking.

As Lent comes closer to an end, review these last five weeks and think about what this time of pausing with the psalms has meant for you. In what ways have you taken time to wait, to notice how God is speaking to you in and through these ancient texts?

Questions for Reflection

1. What lament have you expressed lately?
2. What actions or turnings from what is right need to be named? What injustices need to be called out?
3. Think about a time you have experienced God's forgiveness. How would you describe it?
4. What do you think is the difference between waiting and hoping?
5. What is your experience of waiting for God?

Palm Sunday/Holy Week

Psalm 118: Thanksgiving

I think it's part of my DNA to love a parade. I remember as a child going downtown during the Christmas season. My dad would bring the green kitchen stool so that I could stand on it and be able to see everything over the heads of the crowd. My very tall father would put my little brother on his shoulders so that he could see too. It seemed magical and special to be at such a happy event. I loved the music, the movements, the crowd of happy people being together, and the adventure of going together as a family.

It's probably why I love Palm Sunday. Worshipers wave palm branches, sing, and shout, "Hosanna!" Even churches that may not always include children in worship do so on this festal day in the Christian calendar. Children of all ages are invited to walk or run down the aisle ahead of the choir and clergy waving their palms as the congregation sings, "Hosanna!"

The tradition that I really like is when everyone in the congregation gathers outside the sanctuary and gets a palm branch. Then as the music begins, all join in singing loud hosannas as they wave their palms and enter the sanctuary in a parade with running feet, or feet assisted with chairs, walkers, canes, or even a service dog!

There's something about a parade that brings energy and life, as we give thanks for the community being together, moving, singing, and celebrating. With the Palm Sunday parade, we reenact the story of Jesus' entry into Jerusalem to confront political leaders, holding off for a few moments the difficult days that will follow in Holy Week.

Psalm 118 was used in liturgical processions into the temple in ancient Jerusalem, and Christians regularly hear this psalm read on Palm Sunday. Verse 24 reminds worshipers of the reason for their rejoicing: "This is the day that the LORD has made; let us rejoice and be glad in it" (NRSVue). Perhaps the reciting of this familiar verse telling of God's creative work is just what we need as we move into Holy Week. What is most important to remember? For what are we most thankful? Each of the days in this week provides us with moments of remembering God's work in us and through us as we recall Jesus' life and teachings. The joy and thanksgiving of celebrating Jesus' entry into Jerusalem stays with us and sustains us, even as there are difficult moments ahead.

The invitation of this psalm is to join our voices with friends and family in offering our own prayers of thanksgiving. As we leave the sanctuary with palms in hand, we take with us the joy of the day, rejoicing in the opportunity to give thanks to God for *hesed*—God's faithful love that is freely available.

Attend to Psalm 118

As you read Psalm 118, there are a few things to remember. It is a psalm of thanksgiving, one that was used in early Jewish life as worshipers entered the temple. It is the last of the Hallel or praise psalms (Psalms 113–118) that were read when Jews made pilgrimages to Jerusalem for Passover, Shavuot (when Christians celebrate Pentecost), and Sukkot.

Another interesting fact is that Psalm 118 is the most quoted psalm in the New Testament. All four Gospel writers cite it as they tell the story of Jesus' entry into Jerusalem. As you read it, notice the rhythm of the song and how it moves from individual to communal responses. Pay attention to phrases that are repeated.

Psalm 118 (NRSVue)

A Song of Victory
¹O give thanks to the LORD, for he is good;
    his steadfast love endures forever!

²Let Israel say,
    "His steadfast love endures forever."
³Let the house of Aaron say,
    "His steadfast love endures forever."
⁴Let those who fear the LORD say,
    "His steadfast love endures forever."

⁵Out of my distress I called on the LORD;
    the LORD answered me and set me in a broad place.
⁶With the LORD on my side I do not fear.
    What can mortals do to me?
⁷The LORD is on my side to help me;
    I shall look in triumph on those who hate me.
⁸It is better to take refuge in the LORD
    than to put confidence in mortals.
⁹It is better to take refuge in the LORD
    than to put confidence in princes.

¹⁰All nations surrounded me;
    in the name of the LORD I cut them off!
¹¹They surrounded me, surrounded me on every side;
    in the name of the LORD I cut them off!
¹²They surrounded me like bees;
    they blazed like a fire of thorns;
    in the name of the LORD I cut them off!
¹³I was pushed hard, so that I was falling,
    but the LORD helped me.
¹⁴The LORD is my strength and my might;
    he has become my salvation.

¹⁵There are glad songs of victory in the tents of the righteous:
"The right hand of the LORD does valiantly;
    ¹⁶the right hand of the Lord is exalted;
    the right hand of the LORD does valiantly."
¹⁷I shall not die, but I shall live
    and recount the deeds of the LORD.

¹⁸The LORD has punished me severely,
   but he did not give me over to death.

¹⁹Open to me the gates of righteousness,
   that I may enter through them
   and give thanks to the LORD.

²⁰This is the gate of the LORD;
   the righteous shall enter through it.

²¹I thank you that you have answered me
   and have become my salvation.
²²The stone that the builders rejected
   has become the chief cornerstone.
²³This is the LORD's doing;
   it is marvelous in our eyes.
²⁴This is the day that the LORD has made;
   let us rejoice and be glad in it.
²⁵Save us, we beseech you, O LORD!
   O LORD, we beseech you, give us success!

²⁶Blessed is the one who comes in the name of the LORD.
   We bless you from the house of the LORD.
²⁷The LORD is God,
   and he has given us light.
Bind the festal procession with branches,
   up to the horns of the altar.

²⁸You are my God, and I will give thanks to you;
   you are my God; I will extol you.

²⁹O give thanks to the LORD, for he is good,
   for his steadfast love endures forever.

This thanksgiving hymn begins with the single voice of the individual. Then the one voice joins in with the voices of the community gathered in worship. It has a fairly simple structure. The repetition of the phrase in the call to worship (vv. 1–4) reminds the worshipers of the reason for their thanksgiving. Verses 5–18 form the first major section, in which the voice of the individual is heard describing the situation he is experiencing. The psalmist was in a narrow place, experiencing distress, the hatred of enemies, feelings of being surrounded, and falling. The situation is dire.

The words of the psalmist in verse 14 may be familiar: "The LORD is my strength and my might; he has become my salvation" were repeated by Miriam and Moses and the Israelites as they crossed the Red Sea in Exodus 15. Just as God was with the Israelites as they faced the possibility of death, the psalmist also knows God's saving presence. At the very start of the description of the terrifying situation the psalmist faces is the affirmation "[God] set me in a broad place." The section then concludes with the declaration "But I shall live."

The second major section, verses 19–29, begins with the voice of the individual and then transitions to the voices of the worshiping community in verse 24 with these familiar words: "This is the day that the LORD has made; let us rejoice and be glad in it."

As you read Psalm 118:24 from the different translations and the paraphrases from *The Message* and *The Manhattan Psalter*, notice the similarities and differences of expression.

This is the day the LORD acted;
we will rejoice and celebrate in it!
　　　　　—CEB

This is the day made memorable by Yahweh, what immense joy for us!
　　　　　—*The Jerusalem Bible* (JB)

This is the day that our Source of Joy has made;
Let us exult and rejoice in it.
　　　　　—Pamela Greenberg, *The Complete Psalms*

This is the very day GOD acted—
let's celebrate and be festive!
　　　　　—MSG (paraphrase)

This day was made in heaven, let's enjoy and revel in every minute of it.
—*The Manhattan Psalter: The Lectio Divina of Sister Juanita Colon*
(paraphrase)

This is the day that the LORD has made;
let us rejoice and be glad in it.
—NRSVue

Jews hear this ancient song of the Israelites as they celebrate Sukkot in the fall, when they remember the gathering of the harvest and the exodus from slavery in Egypt. On Palm Sunday, Christians enter the sanctuary waving palms, celebrating and giving thanks for another day that God has provided, as they hear these familiar words of the psalmist read aloud in worship.

In the time of the Israelites, this psalm could have served as a "model prayer for the worshipping community."[1] The psalmist expresses needs to God and, being assured of God's faithful response, offers thanksgiving, vividly describing God as "Source of Joy," the one who has made this day, and made it one in which God has acted.

This faithful psalmist is a witness to God's "involvement in the world and the community of faith," showing how "the individual story of salvation provides an example of God's beneficent engagement with the world."[2] In the articulation of this prayer of thanksgiving, the psalmist then invites the community of worshipers to join in with their voices as they, too, acknowledge God's presence with them.

As faithful witnesses today, Christians read this psalm and speak of the ways God is present and engaged with the world in which we live. As we wave palms and shout "Hosanna!" in praise and thanksgiving, we remember Jesus, who entered Jerusalem to face his enemies and bring life into the death-dealing world.

Connect with Thanksgiving

Two parts of this psalm connect us with a theme of thanksgiving and Palm Sunday. At the beginning of the psalm, the repetition of thanks for God's steadfast love provides an invitation to consider what you have been taught about the nature of God.

Some have grown up with the mistaken teaching that the God of the Old Testament is a God of judgment and revenge. But this psalm attests to God as a God of love, a God who listens and responds, not a God to be feared. In the words of Stephen Montgomery, "God's steadfast love is the very essence of God's character, which is revealed in acts of liberation and deliverance. The Hebrew root of 'steadfast love' is a mother's womb—God's strong, compassionate, fiercely steadfast love."[3] Imagine God's love being that strong, that persistent, that fiercely present in your life.

A second thing to notice in this psalm is verse 5. The CEB translates it this way: "In tight circumstances, I cried out to the LORD. The LORD answered me with wide-open spaces." In *The Message*, Eugene Peterson paraphrases it this way: "Pushed to the wall, I called to GOD; from the wide open spaces, he answered. GOD's now at my side and I'm not afraid; who would dare lay a hand on me?"

How comforting it must have been for the psalmist to know that God was there in the most difficult moments, speaking from a wider space to the psalmist, who was hemmed in by distress and could see no way out. Hearing this psalm on Palm Sunday invites us to connect it with the events that begin Holy Week. The Gospels recount the story of Jesus' entry into Jerusalem, which would have been a very wide place, a place full of activity with pilgrims arriving for Passover. But the wide space Jesus entered quickly became a narrow space as the local officials became determined to shut down his voice.

As we move through the remaining days of Holy Week to Easter Sunday, we can see how this space of God's presence continues to shift, from broad to narrow to broad again through Jesus' life, death, and resurrection. With the psalmist we can say, "This is the day the LORD acted; we will rejoice and celebrate in it!" (CEB).

Pause with Your Heart Each Day

Psalm 118, which is used in Christian worship during Holy Week and the season of Easter, is also read or sung by Jews at Passover. In hearing this familiar psalm, Jews remember the exodus and God's saving acts. And in this remembering, they affirm that God will continue to act.

We start Holy Week with Palm or Passion Sunday. Just as Jesus entered Jerusalem for the last time, we are invited to enter this week, walking with Jesus as we slowly move through Maundy Thursday, Good Friday, and then the celebration of Easter. And we, too, remember the acts of Jesus.

For your activity of pausing this day and for the three days leading up to the last days of Holy Week, try this practice. As you go about your day, be attentive to the places where you see God acting. What acts make you want to celebrate and give thanks? Rather than rushing on with your life, pause and offer a silent prayer of thanks.

Another way to remember God's acts is to take some photographs. Where do you see evidence of things, people, or places for which you are thankful? Take a picture of them. Then on Wednesday, review the photographs you have taken. What themes are evident? What in these images do you want to remember?

Try reading the psalm again and looking at the images you have captured either with your memory or with your camera, lifting your heart in thanks for these signs of God's steadfast love.

Questions for Reflection

1. What is your experience of knowing the steadfast love of God?
2. Recall a time when you were in a tight space and saw no way out. In what ways was God present for you, inviting you into a wider or better place?
3. In what ways have your understandings about the nature of God changed over the years?
4. What words or images would you use to describe your thanksgiving to God?

Reflection for Maundy Thursday

Psalm 116: Listening

Attentive listening is fast becoming a lost art. Think back to the last conversation you had in which you really listened to someone or when someone really listened to you. What do you recall from that experience? How did it feel?

I wonder about this a lot when I eat out with family and friends. There we are sitting around a table, everyone with a phone in a pocket or a purse or on the table next to the napkin. Do you ever wonder or try to remember how we sat at table with each other before we had cell phones? Was our conversation, our listening, more engaged?

It seems as if cell phones are both bane and blessing. They are wonderful to have for directions, for being in immediate contact with each other, and for finding needed information in an instant. But they are a challenge when they get in the way of human connection. I think about how much we miss opportunities for conversation, reflection on the day, connecting with life moments—the kind of listening that forms and nurtures relationships.

The church where I worship in Nashville, Westminster Presbyterian, has a response to the reading of Scripture in worship that I've never experienced anywhere else. Prior to the first reading, the liturgist says, "Hear the word of God!" and the response of the people is "Our ears are open."

Christians often hear Psalm 116 read every Holy Week on this day of remembering Jesus' Last Supper with his disciples during the

Passover. Jews hear it read at some major festivals, but it is especially important when heard at the celebration of Passover, a time of remembering God's merciful presence with them during the exodus. How interesting that this psalm of praise and thanksgiving has a central place in the liturgies of both Jews and Christians during these holy days.

Consider how we listen, what we hear, and how we respond when recalling the meal in the room where Jesus gathered with his disciples around a table for a Passover meal. In remembering this meal, Christians gather on Maundy Thursday around the table at church and recall Jesus' words to his disciples. He gave them a new commandment (*mandatum*): to love one another as he loved them (John 13:34). What did they hear? What do we hear when we listen to Psalm 116 on this day that moves us more deeply into Holy Week? Hopefully our ears are open to the many ways God's presence in our life is noticed, named, and remembered.

Attend to Psalm 116

Psalm 116 is one of the psalms included in the Hallel (Psalms 113–118), which are read on Passover, Shavuot, and Sukkot. It is an individual hymn of thanksgiving. As you read it, notice why the writer is thankful to God and the promises he makes.

Psalm 116 (CEB)

¹I love the LORD because he hears
    my requests for mercy.
²I'll call out to him as long as I live,
    because he listens closely to me.
³Death's ropes bound me;
    the distress of the grave found me—
    I came face-to-face with trouble and grief.
⁴So I called on the LORD's name:
    "LORD, please save me!"

⁵The LORD is merciful and righteous;
    our God is compassionate.

⁶The Lᴏʀᴅ protects simple folk;
    he saves me whenever I am brought down.
⁷I tell myself, You can be at peace again,
    because the Lᴏʀᴅ has been good to you.
⁸You, God, have delivered me from death,
    my eyes from tears,
    and my foot from stumbling,
    ⁹so I'll walk before the Lᴏʀᴅ
    in the land of the living.
¹⁰I have remained faithful, even when I said,
    "I am suffering so badly!"
    ¹¹even when I said, out of fear,
    "Everyone is a liar!"

¹²What can I give back to the Lᴏʀᴅ
    for all the good things he has done for me?
¹³I'll lift up the cup of salvation.
    I'll call on the Lᴏʀᴅ's name.
¹⁴I'll keep the promises I made to the Lᴏʀᴅ
    in the presence of all God's people.
¹⁵The death of the Lᴏʀᴅ's faithful
    is a costly loss in his eyes.

¹⁶Oh yes, Lᴏʀᴅ, I am definitely your servant!
    I am your servant and the son of your female servant—
    you've freed me from my chains.
¹⁷So I'll offer a sacrifice of thanksgiving to you,
    and I'll call on the Lᴏʀᴅ's name.
¹⁸I'll keep the promises I made to the Lᴏʀᴅ
    in the presence of all God's people,
    ¹⁹in the courtyards of the Lᴏʀᴅ's house,
    which is in the center of Jerusalem.

Praise the Lᴏʀᴅ!

Like other individual psalms of thanksgiving, Psalm 116 follows a
simple literary structure. With verses 1–2, the psalmist acknowledges

a love of God. The psalmist knows of God's love in return because God listens and hears all requests. The next part of the psalm, verses 3–11, describes the psalmist's experiences. The NRSVue has given this psalm the title of "Thanksgiving for Recovery from Illness" because of the mention of illness and suffering in verses 8 and 10. The third part of the psalm, verses 12–19, conclude the psalmist's comments with words of promise in thanksgiving for the ways God has listened and acted.

Read how the first two verses of the psalm have been translated or paraphrased below. Pay attention to how God's presence is described.

> I love GOD because he listened to me,
>   listened as I begged for mercy.
> He listened so intently
>   as I laid out my case before him.
>   —MSG (paraphrase)

> Alleluia! I am filled with love when Yahweh listens to the sound
>   of my prayer,
> when he bends down to hear me, as I call.
>   —*The New Jerusalem Bible* (NJB)

> I love the LORD, for He has heard
>   my voice, my supplications.
> For He has inclined His ear to me
>   when in my days I called.
> —Robert Alter, *The Hebrew Bible*,
>   vol. 3, *The Writings* (Ketuvim)

> I love the LORD because he hears
>   my requests for mercy.
> I'll call out to him as long as I live,
>   because he listens closely to me.
>   —CEB

Though they share very common phrasing, these different translations and Peterson's paraphrase in *The Message* provide us with rich images of the psalmist's experience of God's presence and the reason for this song of thanksgiving: God leaned God's ear and "listens closely," "listened intently," "bends down to hear." Notice Robert Alter's translation of verse 2: " For He has inclined His ear to me when in my days I called." In Hebrew the word translated here as "inclined" has the literal meaning of being stretched out.

Two additional observations about this psalm help us see the connections with Maundy Thursday. At the conclusion of the description of the psalmist's difficulties in verse 9, the psalmist writes, "So I'll walk before the LORD in the land of the living" (CEB). In his commentary on this verse, Robert Alter notes that the idiom "walk before the LORD" has a double meaning: "to walk about and to perform service. The speaker, restored to life, will do both."[1]

At the beginning of the third section of the psalm, at verse 12, the psalmist asks, "What can I give back to the LORD for all the good things he has done for me? I'll lift up the cup of salvation. I'll call on the LORD's name" (CEB). The psalmist experiences physical change, moving from a place of trouble, grief, stumbling, and possible death to being able to walk "in the land of the living." So he lifts a cup in worship as an act of thanksgiving and praise to God.

This symbol of the raising of the cup of salvation has a place in the traditions of both Jews and Christians. At the Passover seder, four cups are raised to remember God's saving action at the exodus. In the liturgy of Maundy Thursday, Jesus offers a cup of salvation to his disciples and asks them to remember him.

I'm struck by the promise made by the psalmist in verses 18–19: "I'll complete what I promised GOD I'd do, and I'll do it in company with his people, in the place of worship, in GOD's house, in Jerusalem, GOD's city" (MSG). "I'll keep the promises I made to the LORD in the presence of all God's people, in the courtyards of the LORD's house, which is in the center of Jerusalem" (CEB).

The psalmist makes a sure and certain promise to God. We don't know the content of that promise. It seems to be private. But it would be interesting to speculate. Whatever was promised will be made evident in a very public place in Jerusalem. Perhaps, as Alter suggests, the promise could involve a new resolve for the way the speaker walks "before the LORD." The response of one who has been heard by God and whose life has been restored could result in new ways of walking, new ways of seeing, listening, and serving.

Connect with Listening

Since we know that this psalm is read at Passover, imagine the possibility of Jesus quoting it at the meal he shared with the disciples in the upper room. What do you think they heard? If they had conversation among themselves, what do you imagine they said or heard? What do you think they would remember later after they left that table?

In his commentary on Psalm 116, David J. Wood has observed that often services of worship on Maundy Thursday reflect a very somber tone, one that does not invite "testimonies of thanksgiving" like that which we hear in this psalm, but he counters, "Good Friday eve was and is an occasion for thanksgiving. It is a night for the recovering of stories that give voice to the way in which God has heard and has attended to us as a people born to die and give thanks for the way in which God has become known to us in the particularity of our need. It is a night for testimony. It is a night for acts of dedication."[2]

Read Psalm 116 again, and this time follow it with a reading of Jesus at an evening meal with his disciples (John 13:1–16, 31–35 or Luke 22:7–20) The psalmist testifies to how God's acts of mercy and compassion have restored life when it looked like death was imminent.

The story of Jesus at a meal with his disciples is equally rich in words and imagery. In the act of washing the disciples' feet, of breaking bread and pouring a cup, Jesus invites the disciples to join with him in dedicating their lives to the risky task of following him. Both the psalm and the Gospel stories remind us of the invitation God gives us to "walk about and to perform service."[3] Our lives become a testimony of how well we have listened.

Pause with Your Heart Today

Once when I lived in Chicago, friends noticed that I seemed a bit stressed. They gave me a gift certificate for a massage. I reluctantly acknowledged what they were seeing and made an appointment with the massage therapist. After the massage was done, I was relaxing and talking with the woman who had given me this gift of easing the tension in my neck and shoulders. I noticed a small box on her coffee table. She told me it was a prayer box. In it she kept names of people for whom she was praying. And as she went about her day, she would touch the box as a way to remind her of those whose names were in the box.

Pausing with this psalm on Maundy Thursday during Holy Week offers an invitation to us to consider the ways we listen. Look again at the different ways verses 1–2 have been translated or paraphrased. God is described as one who "listens closely" or "intently" and as one who "bends down" to be near. In his commentary on this psalm, Konrad Schaefer gives it the title "God Listens to Those Who Call."[4]

Thinking about the literal meaning of the Hebrew word translated "inclined" as being stretched out makes me wonder about the physical act of listening. Do we stretch out to hear another? What happens during that moment of stretching out? How is the one who is being heard changed? And, conversely, how is the one who is listening stretched in this encounter?

The practice of intently listening, of being close, is a spiritual practice. It requires time, energy, patience, and presence. Perhaps you have friends or family members who count on you. And you probably have friends whom you can count on to listen to you.

Today, on Maundy Thursday, recall those people who have listened to you this week. Give thanks for their presence in your life. And name those people to whom you have "stretched out" or "listened intently" recently. Recall those people to whom you have listened. On small pieces of paper, write down the names in both groups of people. Place their names in a bowl or small box in a place where you will see them during your day. This simple practice helps keep you walking about, affirming God's presence in your life and the ways God calls you to listen and to act.

Questions for Reflection

1. Imagine yourself at the Passover table with Jesus in the upper room. What do you think you would have heard? What question would you have asked?

2. In the upper room, Jesus invited disciples to share a meal and to receive the gift of having their feet washed. And he reminded them of a new commandment: to love. What stories do you want to recover that testify to the ways these acts are evident today in your life, in the life of your church, or in the life of your community?

3. In what ways have you experienced God listening to your prayers? How are they similar to or different from the experiences of the speaker in this psalm?

4. In what ways are your ears open or closed to those around you?

Reflection for Good Friday

Psalm 22: Being Alone or Abandoned

Recently I was driving from a visit with friends in Florence, Alabama, to my sister's home in Tuscaloosa, following the directions on my phone. Somewhere about two hours into the journey, on a backroad, it dawned on me that if I lost cell phone service, I would have no idea what turn I needed to make. I tried not to panic. I was determined to focus on anything but the number of bars on my phone and wondering if a cell phone tower would appear on the horizon. So I kept driving, hoping and praying the directions would continue and I would not be left abandoned, alone on a country road on a Sunday morning with no one knowing where I was.

The experience of being alone or abandoned is one shared by humans at any age. A baby learning to crawl leaves the room, and a parent hears her cry and goes looking for her. She's crawled just out of sight of her parent and is crying because she suddenly realizes she is alone. She hasn't been forgotten, but all she knows is she can't see the one who loves her.

The feeling of being separated from God whose love is merciful and abounding is the poetic and prayerful expression of the writer of Psalm 22. As we draw near to the end of Holy Week, we arrive at Good Friday. I've always struggled with the title of this day and muse on what's good about a day in the Christian calendar when we recall the death of Jesus on the cross. A quick internet search will tell you that it's called "good" because the death of Jesus by the Roman state makes possible the celebration of Easter and the risen Lord.

Psalm 22 is read on Good Friday in congregational worship. The psalm begins with the cry that is heard on the lips of Jesus as recorded by the Gospel writers Mark and Matthew: "My God, my God, why have you forsaken me?" It's a haunting and raw question from the psalmist and takes on a new intensity when uttered by Jesus from the cross. Psalm 22 invites us in to consider our own questions and experiences of being alone, forsaken, or abandoned—even, as it sometimes feels, by God.

Thankfully, I made it safely on my road trip. The cell phone connection held up. I was even able to listen to my sister preaching on the live stream of her church's worship service. Feeling all alone, fighting a bit of anxiety, I was strangely comforted by technology that worked, by the voice of my sister, by the music and the prayers, and by the community gathered on a Sunday morning virtually and in person, of which I was a part.

Attend to Psalm 22

Psalm 22 has a rich history for both Jews and Christians. Though it is ascribed to David, scholars agree it was not written by him but rather by an anonymous poet, an individual expressing a lament to God. In her commentary on this psalm, Old Testament scholar Esther Menn writes, "Psalm 22 features an especially compelling persona, who gives voice to his or her sense of God's abandonment and anticipation of divine response. It must be emphasized, however, that despite its prominent display of first-person expression, Psalm 22 includes suggestive indications of a surrounding community presence."[1] In the expression of feelings of abandonment and suffering and the painful treatment by enemies, this writer also affirms the presence of the surrounding community. Even in the darkest moment, God's face is not hidden for this psalmist or for the congregation.

As you read this psalm, notice what the writer is saying. What is the lament? Where do you see the writer affirming connections with the community? And finally, what is the writer saying about God?

Psalm 22 (NRSVue)

Plea for Deliverance from Suffering and Hostility
To the leader: according to The Deer of the Dawn. A Psalm of David.

[1]My God, my God, why have you forsaken me?
    Why are you so far from helping me, from the words of my
        groaning?
[2]O my God, I cry by day, but you do not answer;
    and by night but find no rest.

[3]Yet you are holy,
    enthroned on the praises of Israel.
[4]In you our ancestors trusted;
    they trusted, and you delivered them.
[5]To you they cried and were saved;
    in you they trusted and were not put to shame.

[6]But I am a worm and not human,
    scorned by others and despised by the people.
[7]All who see me mock me;
    they sneer at me; they shake their heads;
[8]"Commit your cause to the LORD; let him deliver—
    let him rescue the one in whom he delights!"

[9]Yet it was you who took me from the womb;
    you kept me safe on my mother's breast.
[10]On you I was cast from my birth,
    and since my mother bore me you have been my God.
[11]Do not be far from me,
    for trouble is near,
    and there is no one to help.

[12]Many bulls encircle me;
    strong bulls of Bashan surround me;
[13]they open wide their mouths at me,
    like a ravening and roaring lion.

¹⁴I am poured out like water,
 and all my bones are out of joint;
my heart is like wax;
 it is melted within my breast;
¹⁵my mouth is dried up like a potsherd,
 and my tongue sticks to my jaws;
 you lay me in the dust of death.

¹⁶For dogs are all around me;
 a company of evildoers encircles me;
they bound my hands and feet.
¹⁷I can count all my bones.
They stare and gloat over me;
¹⁸they divide my clothes among themselves,
 and for my clothing they cast lots.

¹⁹But you, O LORD, do not be far away!
 O my help, come quickly to my aid!
²⁰Deliver my soul from the sword,
 my life from the power of the dog!
 ²¹Save me from the mouth of the lion!

From the horns of the wild oxen you have rescued me.
²²I will tell of your name to my brothers and sisters;
 in the midst of the congregation I will praise you:
²³You who fear the LORD, praise him!
 All you offspring of Jacob, glorify him;
 stand in awe of him, all you offspring of Israel!
²⁴For he did not despise or abhor
 the affliction of the afflicted;
he did not hide his face from me
 but heard when I cried to him.

²⁴From you comes my praise in the great congregation;
 my vows I will pay before those who fear him.
²⁶The poor shall eat and be satisfied;
 those who seek him shall praise the LORD.
 May your hearts live forever!

²⁷All the ends of the earth shall remember
and turn to the L<small>ORD</small>,
and all the families of the nations
shall worship before him.
²⁸For dominion belongs to the L<small>ORD</small>,
and he rules over the nations.

²⁹To him, indeed, shall all who sleep in the earth bow down;
before him shall bow all who go down to the dust,
and I shall live for him.
³⁰Posterity will serve him;
future generations will be told about the Lord
³¹and proclaim his deliverance to a people yet unborn,
saying that he has done it.

Notice the beginning of the psalm and the words of being alone and abandoned. Psalm 22 was probably written before the Babylonian exile and the destruction of the temple in Jerusalem. As you read through the psalms, you can see how many of them begin this way. As Walter Brueggemann and William H. Bellinger Jr. note, "A loss of Jerusalem and the sixth century displacement became for Israel the quintessential moment of divine abandonment, and we imagine this and many psalms like it in such a context."[2]

Psalm 22 follows the form of an individual song of complaint or lament, which usually has these elements: address to God of specific complaints, request to God for help, affirmation that God will hear and respond. The psalmist is in such distress that the complaint to God begins with the first verse.

Abraham Jacob Berkovitz says, "Psalm 22 provided a colorful [palette] with which ancient Jews and early Christians painted."[3] In preparation for looking at the brushstrokes used by people of faith working with this wide-ranging palette of poetic expression, take a few moments to look more specifically at verses 1–2 and 19 from different translations and paraphrases.

God, God . . . my God!
Why did you dump me

miles from nowhere?
Doubled up with pain, I call to God
all the day long. No answer. Nothing.
. . . .
You, GOD—don't put off my rescue!
Hurry and help me!

                    —MSG (paraphrase)

My God, my God, why have You forsaken me?
    Far from my rescue are the words that I roar.
. . . .
But You, O LORD, be not far.

                    —Robert Alter, *The Hebrew Bible*,
                        vol. 3, *The Writings* (Ketuvim)

My God! My God,
    why have you left me all alone?
    Why are you so far from saving me—
        so far from my anguished groans?
. . . .
But you, LORD! Don't be far away!
    You are my strength!
    Come quick and help me!

                    —CEB

My God, my God, why have you forsaken me?
You keep yourself distant from my cries,
words that I roar out in pain.
. . . .
But you are God—don't be distant!
    —Pamela Greenberg, *The Complete Psalms*

Oh God, God, where are you? Why don't you answer me? Have
you so utterly abandoned me that you can't even hear my cries for
help? . . . Father, please help me or I'm finished.

        —*The Manhattan Psalter: The Lectio Divina of Sister Juanita Colon*
                        (paraphrase)

In the first words of this psalm, the writer asks the "why" question about God's absence. The psalmist feels "forsaken," "all alone," "abandoned," dumped "miles from nowhere," waiting to hear a word, an answer from God, something. Then after describing the anguish and experience of being set upon by those who seek to bring harm, the writer regains a more sure place of faith with a plea to God in verse 19: "Hurry and help me," "be not far," "come quick and help me," "don't be distant," "help me or I'm finished."

The "why" question that begins the lament turns in the latter part of the psalm to a plea for God's presence. Sometimes our "why" questions for God hang out there, lingering, with no answers in sight. Other times in our pausing with these questions, we begin to find helpful reassurances that we are not alone.

In their discussion of this psalm and how it is read and understood by Jews and Christians, Amy-Jill Levine and Marc Zvi Brettler have wisely observed, "The psalm speaks to horror and danger, but it speaks to more than that. It allows us to express the feeling that any of us have had—that God has abandoned us. At the same time, it ironically insists that we have not abandoned the relationship. A lament psalm is a poem of raw honesty and fidelity. It is appropriate on the lips of Jesus the Jew, and anyone who feels abandoned by God."[4]

On this Good Friday, a reading of Psalm 22 connects us not only with the final moments of Jesus' life but also with our own moments of feeling separated from God. The psalmist pleads with God, "Do not be far from me, for trouble is near, and there is no one to help" (v. 11) and then later writes that God heard and God's face was not hidden in those moments the psalmist cried out to God (v. 24). We are left at the end of the psalm, as Brettler and Levine observe, with the "raw honesty and fidelity"[5] of the psalmist's hymn, the stories of Jesus' last breaths, our own experiences of feeling alone and abandoned, and an ongoing confidence that God ultimately remains with us.

Connect with Being Alone or Abandoned

I love the book of Psalms for many reasons, but one of the main ones is that its expressions of joy, thanksgiving, and lament voiced as individuals and acknowledged within community are still relevant today.

This psalm of lament is hard to read, however. One wonders if it needs a warning label. But then when read on Good Friday in light of the Gospel accounts of Jesus' death in Mark, it takes on a particular meaning for Christians. The psalm works its mosaic of feelings in the reader, feelings that are both individual and communal, expressions of an ancient poet writing as the contemporary reader knows the destruction of the temple in Jerusalem looms. We can be transported in time to help us understand the suffering of Jesus, as well as our own suffering.

Biblical scholar Ellen Davis wonders if Christians have familiarity with lament psalms since so few are read in worship. She also notes the difference between contemporary practices of prayer among churchgoers and those of ancient Israelites, who believed that "the kind of prayer in which we most need fluency is the loud groan."[6]

Consider your own practices of prayer. Did you grow up experiencing prayer at mealtimes, at bedtime, or in spontaneous moments of awe and thanksgiving, like "Thank you, God, for this beautiful sunset"? A foundation of faith is laid when prayer is experienced as a daily practice, weaving together the moments of our lives with our sense of God. And this daily life we experience is not without challenges, frustrations, and times of deep sadness when we, too, want to say to God, "Why?" or "Where are you?" or "Why did this happen to me?" or "Why are you so far away, God?" or "Why am I left alone to suffer?" Our laments join those of the psalm writer. Without a basic foundation of faith that has honed an awareness of God with us day-to-day, it can be harder to deal with the feeling of the absence of God. But God is not shocked or offended by our feelings, and our feelings don't mean a failure of faith. Whether they are soothed quickly or remain with us for a long time, we can do our best to say that God's care and steadfast love are still with us.

This psalm can awaken us to the power of lament, the necessity of sometimes letting out a "loud groan" to God. God can handle our "why" questions, and God will surround us with mercy, kindness, and abiding love.

Pause with Your Heart Today

We live in a world where the psalmist's words of lament written so long ago are still ours today. The fears of the writer about bulls, dogs, lions, and wild oxen—metaphors for forces that threaten life—can easily be translated into the things that cause us fear today. One wonders what happened to cause the psalmist to experience such deep anguish. The voice of one who is going through the depths of grief and pain, of separation from God who is the source of life, is expressed in these verses: "I am poured out like water, and all my bones are out of joint; my heart is like wax; it is melted within my breast." Honest, raw, difficult, hard—this psalm, so deeply human, invites our own laments.

> Think of the people you know who have said the words that begin the psalm: "My God, my God, why have you forsaken me?"
>
> Think of the racism in our country that has allowed and continues to allow the murders of African Americans, Asians, Jews, and others in the past and today: "My God, my God, why have you forsaken me?"
>
> Think of people living in abusive situations who feel as if they have no hope of ever getting out: "My God, my God, why have you forsaken me?"
>
> Think of students in schools and on college campuses learning how to "run, hide, fight" as gun violence increases in our country: "My God, my God, why have you forsaken me?"
>
> Think of our youth and young adults whose very lives are at risk because of anti-LGBTQ legislation: "My God, my God, why have you forsaken me?"

What are your laments? Take some time this day to name your "loud groans." If you journal, write them down. If you enjoy walking outside, name them with your steps. If you are able to be in worship with a faith community, read this psalm before you go. When you hear it read in worship, silently name the bulls, lions, dogs, and wild oxen that surround you or someone you know.

Then as you end this day, let your lament slowly turn to thanksgiving. Give thanks for the ways God's sustaining presence has been with you and others who are suffering. Give thanks for the ways your faith community or your community of family and friends surrounds you with love. Give thanks as you look for God's deliverance and justice for those in extremely difficult situations, and seek how you can help demonstrate God's presence in these situations through your actions.

Questions for Reflection

1. What is your lament, your "loud groan"?
2. When was a time you felt distant from God's presence in your life?
3. Whom do you know who struggles with feeling alone, separated either from God or from a community of support?
4. In what ways is God making God's face visible to you, especially in times of trial?

Reflection for Easter

Psalm 19: Hands

L ent had just begun in 2020 when churches shut down because of COVID and began to move to streaming worship online. It was abrupt and challenging. Smaller churches had little if any budgets for the technology that was required: cameras, screens, microphones. Everyone was scrambling to figure out how to be church, how to continue in ministry within the church and in the community, as everything shifted online. We all thought, "Oh, we will be back together by Pentecost." Pentecost came and went. "Oh, we will be back together by Advent." Advent, Christmas, and Epiphany came and went.

Then it was Lent again in 2021. Pastors and educators offered Lent bags so that families could journey through the season together with educational and liturgical resources to use at home. Ash Wednesday was drive-through at the church. Cars pulled up, and pastors marked the people in the car with the sign of the cross on their foreheads or hands and blessed them. We all thought we would have been back together by then. And Easter was coming, as it blessedly always does.

My sister, who is a pastor, and her choir director decided to take a risk and worship together outside in the courtyard for Easter Sunday, April 4, 2021. It had been a long year of seeing no children, teenagers, or adults in worship, and they thought it would be safe. If everyone came masked and sat distanced, it just might work. And of course, prayers were offered for the weather to cooperate.

We needed a warm sunny day. And it happened just as we had hoped. The joyous reunion of a faith community who had not seen each other in over a year was something to behold. The sun was shining. The light in everyone's eyes could be seen above the masks, which you knew were hiding the biggest smiles! Beloved dogs roamed through the crowd. Muffled voices joined together singing, "Christ the Lord is risen today!" And never had it sounded more beautiful.

The familiar Gospel text from John 20 that we all know by heart was read. The preacher preached and prayed. At the end, everyone shared confetti eggs (cascarones), and the courtyard was covered with colorful confetti and the joyous sounds of a faith community shouting, "The Lord is risen. He is risen indeed!" Our hearts had never been more full than on this Easter Sunday.

Psalm 19 is one of the many readings that is suggested for the service of worship known as the Easter Vigil, which takes place after sundown on the night before Easter. It is a beautifully crafted hymn of praise to God the creator, ending with the prayer that is often used before Scripture is read on Sunday morning. Reading and considering the words and images in the psalm provide a poetic connection with the joy and celebration of Easter Sunday.

Attend to Psalm 19

Psalm 19 provides an evocative conclusion for our journey together as we have paused with the psalms during Lent. As you read it, notice how the psalmist describes the way that God is revealed. And as you come to the familiar words in verse 14, let them become your prayer as you think about the psalm's meaning for you on this Easter Sunday.

Psalm 19 (NRSVue)

God's Glory in Creation and the Law
To the leader. A Psalm of David.

> [1]The heavens are telling the glory of God,
>   and the firmament proclaims his handiwork.

²Day to day pours forth speech,
    and night to night declares knowledge.
³There is no speech, nor are there words;
    their voice is not heard;
⁴yet their voice goes out through all the earth
    and their words to the end of the world.

In the heavens he has set a tent for the sun,
⁵which comes out like a bridegroom from his wedding canopy,
    and like a strong man runs its course with joy.
⁶Its rising is from the end of the heavens
    and its circuit to the end of them,
    and nothing is hid from its heat.

⁷The law of the LORD is perfect,
    reviving the soul;
the decrees of the LORD are sure,
    making wise the simple;
⁸the precepts of the LORD are right,
    rejoicing the heart;
the commandment of the LORD is clear,
    enlightening the eyes;
⁹the fear of the LORD is pure,
    enduring forever;
the ordinances of the LORD are true
    and righteous altogether.
¹⁰More to be desired are they than gold,
    even much fine gold;
sweeter also than honey
    and drippings of the honeycomb.

¹¹Moreover, by them is your servant warned;
    in keeping them there is great reward.
¹²But who can detect one's own errors?
    Clear me from hidden faults.
¹³Keep back your servant also from the insolent;
    do not let them have dominion over me.

> Then I shall be blameless
>   and innocent of great transgression.
>
> [14]Let the words of my mouth and the meditation of my heart
>   be acceptable to you,
>   O LORD, my rock and my redeemer.

In this psalm, the writer is expressing her understanding of how God is known in creation (vv. 1–6) and in the goodness of the law, the Torah (vv. 7–13), which in Hebrew means "instruction." Notice how she describes what the heavens are doing: telling, proclaiming, declaring knowledge, pouring forth speech. All this description of God's glory is done without actual speech, words, or voice. These opening verses invite the reader then and now to pay attention to God's "handiwork," to notice the way God is revealed in space and in time and in creation.

The second part of the psalm then turns to how God is known in the goodness of the law. The law is described as perfect, sure, right, clear, pure, and true. In addition to describing the law in these ways, the psalmist continues by declaring that the laws of God are things to be desired, "sweeter also than honey."

It is important to remember how the Torah functions for Jews. It is not just a list of laws. Rather, as Mark Stanger explains, "it is a template for exodus living in covenant as God's free and faithful people. It is a pattern of life individually embraced and shared with the community as a guide and goal."[1] Jews remember God's first covenant with Noah and God's covenants with Abraham and Moses. The memory of those covenants and the keeping of Torah are formative for their living. When the psalmist keeps the law close, in the heart and in action—God's direction to stay in close relationship with God and to love one's neighbor as oneself—it revives the soul and helps the heart rejoice.

Verses 11–13 reveal the psalmist's confession of failure in hidden faults, insolence, or proud thoughts and include a request for God's abiding presence and help. In his commentary on this psalm, Konrad Schaefer notices, "The poet prays that God's *tôrâh* be the guiding principle in life, that she or he find favor with God and not stray. It provides the means by which a person may be saved from wrong doing."[2]

The beauty of this psalm can be seen in how the psalmist weaves together fairly seamlessly the ways God's self is revealed in nature and in law. Schaefer has observed how in this psalm "the cosmic and moral orders are complementary spheres of God's design; the two can be contemplated in the visible world and with the moral fiber of the heart."[3] Psalm 19 concludes with a summary of the effect of Torah for the psalmist—words for outward expression and the meditations of the heart that sustain the interior soul.

Consider these translations and paraphrases of the first verses of Psalm 19.

> Heaven is declaring God's glory;
>   the sky is proclaiming his handiwork.
> One day gushes the news to the next,
>   and one night informs another what needs to be known.
> Of course, there's no speech, no words—
>   their voices can't be heard—
> but their sound extends throughout the world;
>   their words reach the ends of the earth.
>
> God has made a tent in heaven for the sun.
>   —CEB

> The heavens tell God's glory,
>   and His handiwork sky declares.
> Day to day breathes utterance
>   and night to night pronounces knowledge.
> There is no utterance and there are no words,
>   their voice is never heard.
> Through all the earth their voice goes out,
>   to the world's edge, their words.
> For the sun He set up a tent in them—
>   —Robert Alter, *The Hebrew Bible*, vol. 3,
>   *The Writings* (Ketuvim)

God's glory is on tour in the skies,
    God-craft on exhibit across the horizon.
Madame Day holds classes every morning,
    Professor Night lectures each evening.

Their words aren't heard,
    their voices aren't recorded,
But their silence fills the earth:
    unspoken truth is spoken everywhere.

God makes a huge dome
    for the sun—a superdome!
                —MSG (paraphrase)

The glory of God is blazoned across the heavens, everything
    shouts his name.
Days pass on the glad tidings to one another, nights take it up
and fling it joyously one to the next. Though not a word is uttered,
not a sound reaches us, yet the silence of the heavens is thunderous
with praise. A jubilant message encircles the earth like a golden
ring.
                —*The Manhattan Psalter, The Lectio Divina*
                of Sister Juanita Colon (paraphrase)

For the poet who wrote Psalm 19, God's handiwork is on display in
the skies for all to see. In her paraphrase, Sister Juanita Colon writes
how everything shouts God's name. Eugene Peterson's paraphrase
describes how "God-craft" is seen in the sky where "Madame Day"
and "Professor Night" hold classes but their words aren't heard.

There are no words, no speech, no utterance, yet "their sound
extends throughout the world" (CEB). So God's creating work, God's
crafting, God's handiwork reveal God's story and God's presence in
silence. Just as it was heard by its original audience, Psalm 19 invites
contemporary readers to pause to appreciate God's handiwork—and
maybe, just maybe, to do so in silence.

Connect with Hands

Following the liturgical seasons of the church year provides a welcome rhythm to my spiritual life and a simple and life-sustaining way for moving through the year. It's probably even accurate to say that it provides a life-*challenging* way to move through the year.

Lent has ended. For you, it may have been a time of giving up something or taking up something, but now we go forward into the season of Easter with a most joyous celebration. On Easter Sunday, our attention is focused on the resurrection accounts in the Gospels. Our ears are attuned to hearing those stories as we celebrate the risen Christ. But mingled with those stories of resurrection during the Easter season are questions about what is coming next, for the disciples and for us.

Reading and reflecting on Psalm 19 offers us perspective as we consider the "what next." We are not unlike the people walking on the road to Emmaus, revisiting the events that had just happened in Jerusalem and wondering what was to come. What's next for my life of faith? How am I changed by the events of Holy Week? What consistency is there between "the words of my mouth," "the meditations of my heart," and how I live in the world?

Look again at *The Message*'s paraphrase of verses 1–2 and the psalmist's description of God's creative work: "God's glory is on tour in the skies, God-craft on exhibit across the horizon." The evidence of God's abiding presence is all around us. It's there for us to notice and name! Many translations call this God's "handiwork"—evoking an image of God as an artist personally fashioning with God's own hands the beautiful, expansive sky surrounding us.

This psalm also reminds us that following God's laws is not restrictive but rather a way of knowing what Konrad Schaefer calls "God's loving, solicitous will."[4] The two parts of this psalm invite our own consideration of how we see God as creator—as an active, personal being revealed in the created world and in the sacred story of the world around us and in our own lives, which have been shaped by the righteousness of God that is as beautiful as God's creation.[5] We experience God's presence in psalms like this one, reminding us of both the beauty and the justice of God—who God is, and how God acts on behalf of those who have not experienced fair treatment.

Celebrating the risen Christ doesn't conclude our sacred story. Rather, it's an invitation to life, to living in ways that Jesus taught, a new chapter in our stories, lived in response to Jesus' commandment to love unconditionally. On Easter, we join our hearts in proclaiming the risen Christ whose invitation to live differently awakens us to all the possibilities we have in front of us for using our hands. It took many hands to help churches survive the pandemic. So, too, the work of our hands as Easter people continue to be needed in the communities in which we live. We face the world that God has created. We remember and celebrate the risen Christ by seeking those times and places where our hands continue his care for the world and all its inhabitants.

Pause with Your Heart Today

The first practice that was suggested for Ash Wednesday was a breath prayer, a prayer that you can say in one breath. The concluding verses of Psalm 19, which may be familiar to you, could also be used as a breath prayer: "Let the words of my mouth and the meditation of my heart be acceptable to you, O LORD, my rock and my redeemer." Try saying and pausing after each phrase:

> *"Let the words of my mouth . . ."* Think about the words you have said this day either to yourself or in conversation. Were there words that could have been hurtful? What words were comforting? What words needed to be said to address injustice?
>
> *". . . and the meditations of my heart . . ."* Listen to your heart and the things that have been silently and maybe not so silently waiting there. What are you contemplating or meditating on? Is it a person, a situation?
>
> *". . . be acceptable to you, O LORD, my rock and my redeemer."* In what ways could your words or meditations change so that God would see them as pleasing or helpful or useful in the world? The psalmist affirms God as rock and redeemer. What words would you use to describe God's presence in your life?

Now try saying these verses silently together as a breath prayer. Take a deep breath and repeat one phrase, then breathe out and say the next. You can use the words as the psalmist has written them or paraphrase them as you would like.

Each chapter of this Lenten study has suggested a way to connect a psalm with a particular spiritual practice. As you move into the rest of the Easter season, you may want to revisit some of those practices, both as you care for your spiritual well-being and cultivate your relationship with God and as you listen for how God is calling you to use your gifts, your skills, and your hands to work out God's righteousness on behalf of others.

Questions for Reflection

1. What do you notice in creation that reveals God's handiwork?
2. What connections can you see between Psalm 19 and Easter?
3. In what ways does your life story reveal God's presence in your life?
4. Where are your hands needed in the work of your church, your community, the world?

Leader's Guides

Ash Wednesday Leader's Guide

Psalm 51: A Clean Heart

Preparing to Teach

This is a leader's guide for a one-hour discussion. The time frames are only suggestions to guide you. As you begin this Lenten study, think about how you can make it a safe space for honest conversation about these psalms and participants' individual responses and experiences. Consider the space where you are meeting. Purple is the liturgical color used during Lent. A simple piece of purple cloth or a purple scarf could be placed on a table with a candle, either a pillar candle or a small battery-operated votive candle. You will read a psalm and discuss it each week. Ask participants to bring Bibles with them to class, and also provide copies on the table. Two good translations to have available are the Common English Bible and the New Revised Standard Version Updated Edition. You could also consider having a Jewish translation, such as Paula Greenberg's *The Complete Psalms*.

Notice (10 minutes)

As people are gathering, have this question before them on a screen or on a flipchart or whiteboard:

What has been your experience of Lent and Ash Wednesday?

Collect responses and open with a prayer.

Attend (30 minutes)

• Provide a brief introduction to the psalm using information that is available in the "Attend" section of the Ash Wednesday chapter (pp. 7–8). Include information about the authorship of the psalms being studied and how many of them have been ascribed to David, even though he most likely was not the author. You may also show the introductory video for this chapter (found at www.wjkbooks.com/Pause).

• Ask someone in the group to read aloud Psalm 51. Have the following questions available for all to see, and invite participants to think about their responses as they hear the psalm being read and/or follow along in their Bibles:

  1. How does the psalmist describe God's character in the opening verses?
  2. What is the psalmist saying about himself? What is he asking God to be or do?

• Have the illustrated sheet for Ash Wednesday/Psalm 51 available for everyone to see, either projected or printed (download at www.wjkbooks.com/Pause). Ask different members of the group to read them in turn. Then discuss these two questions:

  1. What are the similarities and differences you notice?
  2. Which one or ones are you drawn to? Why?

Connect (15 minutes)

In his paraphrase of Psalm 51, Eugene Peterson asks God to "shape a Genesis week from the chaos of my life." Discuss these questions:

  1. David asked God for a clean heart. What would a clean heart look like for you?
  2. Have you ever wanted a fresh start, a do-over? Share what you can about that time.
  3. What would a "Genesis week" look like for you?

4. As you look at the images surrounding the translations and paraphrases of Psalm 51, how do they connect with the psalm? In what ways do they speak to your heart?

Pause (5 minutes)

• Invite participants to try the spiritual practice of a heart prayer or a breath prayer each day in the coming week with Psalm 51:10, using one of the translations or paraphrases read today.

• Close by listening to Malcom Guite read his poem *"Miserere mei, Deus."* Audio can be found on Malcolm Guite's website: https://malcolmguite.files.wordpress.com/2020/10/miserere -mei.m4a.

Artist's Reflection

Leigh Aiken, the artist who has provided the images for the online art resource sheets, reflects on what she was thinking as she created the illustrations:

Place your hand on your heart. Feel its beating. Notice the rhythm. A breath prayer is one that can be repeated in one breath. Let Psalm 51:10 be a breath prayer for you. I took this invitation by Elizabeth quite literally when creating this illustration. Indeed, our beating hearts are already an incredible and constant example of cleansing, regenerating, and restoring. Perhaps all we need is to lift our hands to our hearts and be reminded of the miracle of renewal that is already inside each of us.

First Week of Lent Leader's Guide

Psalm 25: Paths

Preparing to Teach

Read over this guide and make note of anything you need to do to get ready to teach this session. If participants are not bringing Bibles with them, then have copies available on the table so that they can follow along as the psalm is being read.

Notice (10 minutes)

As people are gathering, have these questions available on a screen or on a flipchart or whiteboard:

> Is there a path you have followed through life that has been consistent?
>
> Has there been a path you have followed that has taken you in unexpected directions?

Collect responses and open with a prayer, either by you or one of the participants.

Attend (30 minutes)

• Provide an introduction to the psalm using information that is available in the "Attend" section of the First Week of Lent chapter (p. 18). You may also show the introductory video for this chapter (found at www.wjkbooks.com/Pause). Use the responses to the questions above as a segue into a discussion of Psalm 25. Sometimes the paths we follow in life are clear, and sometimes they are not as obvious, so we need help. This psalm is read on the first Sunday in Lent, and the heading tells us that it is attributed to David in a time in his life when he was asking for guidance and deliverance.

• Hear Psalm 25 read by someone in the group. Have these questions available for all to see, and invite participants to think about their responses as they hear the psalm being read and/or follow along in their Bibles.

  1. What is the psalmist asking for from God?
  2. What are some themes present in this psalm? What do you hear David confessing or acknowledging?

• Have the illustrated sheet for the First Week of Lent/Psalm 25 available for everyone to see, either projected or printed (download at www.wjkbooks.com/Pause). Ask different members of the group to read them in turn. Then discuss these two questions:

  1. What are the similarities and differences you notice?
  2. Which one or ones are you drawn to? Why?

Connect (15 minutes)
Look at Pamela Greenberg's translation of Psalm 25:4, 8–9 as you invite discussion of these questions:

  1. What do you think it means when we are attentive to God's teaching "the holy road"? What does a holy road look like?
  2. Can you name someone who has modeled a path of justice for you?

Pause (5 minutes)

• Project or have available copies of the online resource sheet with the questions for reflection and discussion. Invite participants to sit in silence for a few minutes reflecting on their responses to any of the following:

1. Now that you've read this prayer for guidance and deliverance, write down or say your own prayers to God for leading or for rescue.
2. What would a friendship with God look like for you?
3. What guidance are you seeking from God as you follow a path during this Lenten season?

• The spiritual practice suggested for this week in the "Pause with Your Heart" section of this chapter (pp. 24–25) is following a labyrinth. You can read part of that section to participants and invite them to participate in this way each day during this first week of Lent.
• Close with prayer or a reading of Psalm 25:20–21.

Additional Resource

Wendell Berry has a lovely poem about a road, "There Is a Day," in his book *A Timbered Choir*. It can be found through a Google search or accessed at https://twitter.com/WendellDaily/status /876065701668192256?s=20.

Second Week of Lent Leader's Guide

Psalm 27: Faces

Preparing to Teach

Read over the guide, and make note of anything you need to do to get ready to teach this session. If participants are not bringing Bibles with them, have copies available so that they can follow along as the psalm is being read. If you would like to use the suggestion for closing the session, have art supplies available on the table.

Notice (10 minutes)

As people are gathering, have these questions available on a screen or on a flipchart or whiteboard:

> When you think about God's face, what do you see?
> What is it like for you when you can see only people's eyes above the mask they are wearing?

Collect responses and open with a prayer, either by you or one of the participants.

Attend (30 minutes)

- Provide a brief introduction to the psalm using information that is available in the "Attend" section of the Second Week of Lent chapter (p. 28). You may also show the introductory

video for this chapter (found at www.wjkbooks.com/Pause).
Note that this is another psalm attributed to David, one that
expresses the psalmist's confidence in God.
- The psalm has a very noticeable structure. Ask two people
  to read the psalm, one to read verses 1–6 (expression of the
  psalmist's confidence in God) and another to read verses 7–14
  (the psalmist's requests of God). Ask the participants to notice
  the difference in these two sections of the psalm.
- Invite discussion of these questions:

  1. What is your title for Psalm 27?
  2. Does "Triumphant Song of Confidence" fit, or does something
     else seem more appropriate to you?

- Have the illustrated sheet for the Second Week of Lent/Psalm
  27 available for everyone to see, either projected or printed
  (download at www.wjkbooks.com/Pause). Hear them read,
  and then discuss these questions:

  1. What are the similarities and differences you notice?
  2. If you could complete this sentence, what would you say or
     write: *My heart says . . .*

Connect (15 minutes)
Have the online resource sheet with the questions for reflection and
discussion printed or available for viewing on-screen. Discuss these
questions:

  1. What are David's petitions to God in verses 7–14? In what ways
     are these petitions similar to or different from yours?
  2. The Old Testament has stories of Moses, Elijah, and others who
     either saw or wanted to see God's face. And here the psalmist
     equates seeing God's face with God's presence near him. When
     have you had an experience like the psalmist of sensing God's
     face being near to you?

3. Have you ever wondered about God's face, what it looks like? If God's face is turned toward you or toward your church or toward our world, what does God see?
4. Who are the faces God sees and loves that you don't see?

These questions can also be used if appropriate for your group:

1. Where are you struggling with doubt? What are your fears?
2. As you think about this time in your life of faith, for what are you most grateful?

Pause (5 minutes)

The spiritual practice that is suggested for this week is writing or illustrating a psalm in response to Psalm 27. Have available art supplies, such as paper, crayons, water colors, and colored markers. Invite participants to use any of them as they listen to a choral version of this psalm. (Search for "Psalm 27" by Heather Sorenson.) Play it through twice, and then close with prayer.

Third Week of Lent Leader's Guide

Psalm 63: Blessing

Preparing to Teach

Read over this guide, and make note of anything you need to do to get ready to teach this session. If participants are not bringing Bibles with them, have copies available so that they can follow along as the psalm is being read.

Notice (10 minutes)

As people are gathering, have this question available on a screen or on a flipchart or whiteboard:

What are some blessings you have received this week?

After receiving their responses, open with a prayer, either by you or one of the participants.

Attend (30 minutes)

- Provide a brief introduction to the psalm using information that is available in the "Attend" section of the Third Week of Lent chapter (pp. 38–39). You may also show the introductory video for this chapter (found at www.wjkbooks.com/Pause). Note the attribution of this psalm to David and its connection with a wilderness time in his life, as well as the different expressions of this psalmist: longing for God (vv. 1–2); praise and blessing (vv. 3–5); and David's/the psalmist's confidence in God's presence (vv. 6–8).

- Invite someone to read Psalm 63 and for everyone else to listen for the phrases that are used to describe why the psalmist's soul is satisfied.
- Have the illustrated sheet for the Third Week of Lent/Psalm 63 available for everyone to see, either projected or printed (found at www.wjkbooks.com/Pause). Hear them read, and then discuss these questions:

1. What are the similarities and differences you notice?
2. What in these translations and paraphrase help you consider the ways you trust in God?

Connect (15 minutes)

Have the online resource sheet with the questions for reflection and discussion printed or available for viewing on-screen. Use these questions to help participants connect their experiences with those the writer describes in this psalm. This psalmist offers us a window into his belief about God's presence in his life.

1. As you reflect on your life experiences, what are some ways that you have blessed God, or what are some ways that God has blessed you?
2. Has there been a time in your life when you have felt separated from God's presence, a wilderness time like that described by David/the psalmist? What was that experience like?
3. God's presence can be experienced in our daily activities. God's presence is also known to us in the ways that friends, families, and even strangers bless our lives. When have you experienced this kind of presence or blessing?

Pause (5 minutes)

The translators and interpreters of Psalm 63 have suggested we bless God with our whole lives, with every breath we take. We bless God as long as we are alive. Invite participants to pause with this for just a moment.

The spiritual practice that is recommended for this week is *lectio divina*. Remind participants to try this practice each day this week using Psalm 63. Invite them to hear the psalm read again three times, and use the prompts provided for listening for a word, an image, and the invitation God is offering. Close this session with a prayer.

Fourth Week of Lent Leader's Guide

Psalm 23: Tables

Preparing to Teach

Read over this guide, and make note of anything you need to do to get ready to teach this session. If participants are not bringing Bibles with them, have copies available so that they can follow along as the psalm is being read.

Notice (10 minutes)

As people are gathering, have these questions available on a screen or on a flipchart or whiteboard:

> What are some of your memories of Psalm 23? Did you learn it as a child?
> On what occasions do you remember it being read?

After collecting responses, open with a prayer.

Attend (30 minutes)

- Provide a brief introduction to the psalm using information that is available in the "Attend" section of the Fourth Week of Lent chapter (p. 46). You may also show the introductory video for this chapter (found at www.wjkbooks.com/Pause). Include these points described in the study: the center of the psalm ("you are with me"); the psalmist's use of the image of God as shepherd and its meaning; the literary moves made in this beautiful poem.

• Ask someone to read Psalm 23.
• Invite responses to these questions:

1. Which part of this psalm speaks to you?
2. When has this psalm been a comfort for you?

• Have the illustrated sheet for the Fourth Week of Lent/Psalm 23 available for everyone to see, either projected or printed (found at www.wjkbooks.com/Pause). Consider these recent translations and a paraphrase of Psalm 23:5. In what ways do they invite your reflection on the table God sets before us? Hear them read, and then discuss these questions:

1. What are the similarities and differences you notice?
2. What in these translations and paraphrase help you think about what it means to sit at a table facing enemies or fears?

Connect (15 minutes)

Have the online resource sheet with the questions for reflection and discussion printed or available for viewing on-screen. Use these questions to help participants connect their experiences with those of the psalmist:

1. The psalmist writes, "The LORD is my shepherd." How would you complete the sentence "The Lord is my . . ."?
2. What stories from experiences at tables help you connect with Psalm 23?
3. When has God's mercy found you?
4. What promise do you read in Psalm 23? What's the challenge? What's the invitation for you?

Pause (5 minutes)

The spiritual practice that is suggested for this fourth week of Lent is the Examen. Invite participants to try it this week. Introduce this practice by using it to close the session.

• Light a candle or turn on a battery-operated votive candle. As you do this, invite everyone to silently come into God's presence.
• Move through the steps of the Examen with these prompts:

    1. Recall this past week or just yesterday. Silently name some events or interactions you remember.

    2. Review the day more deeply. Where did you see or experience a sense of God's love? Where did you notice God's presence?

    3. Now think about those moments you would like to revisit or do over. Where or when did you not feel the presence of God as closely as you wanted?

    4. Look ahead to the next day and the opportunities it may offer you to experience God's presence in your life. In what ways can you share God's light and love with another?

• Close in prayer.

Fifth Week of Lent Leader's Guide

Psalm 130: Waiting

Preparing to Teach

Read over this guide, and make note of anything you need to do to get ready to teach this session. If participants are not bringing Bibles with them, have copies available so that they can follow along as the psalm is being read. Have a pot of dirt and a packet of seeds on the table. If you would like to assemble seed pots as a group, bring the supplies described in the "Pause" section of the guide.

Notice (10 minutes)

As people are gathering, have this question available on a screen or printed on a flipchart or whiteboard:

What experiences have you had with waiting, big and small?

After gathering some responses, open with a prayer.

Attend (30 minutes)

- Provide a brief introduction to the psalm using information that is available in the "Attend" section of the Fifth Week of Lent chapter (p. 57). You may also show the introductory video for this chapter (found at www.wjkbooks.com/Pause). Include the kind of psalm it is and where it would have been heard by the original audience. Ask the participants to listen for the laments that the poet is expressing.

• Since there are four sections to the psalm, four readers could take turns, with each reading two verses. Pause after each set of two verses and discuss what the psalmist is saying.

• Have the illustrated sheet for the Fifth Week of Lent/Psalm 130 available for everyone to see, either projected or printed (found at www.wjkbooks.com/Pause). Discuss how verses 5–6 in other translations and a paraphrase provide a richness of engagement with this penitential psalm. Pause with each one to notice what is similar and how they differ.

Connect (15 minutes)

Have the online resource sheet with the questions for reflection and discussion printed or available for viewing on-screen. Use these questions to help participants connect the psalm with their lives of faith:

1. What lament have you expressed lately?
2. One of the interesting things to note in the study is the phrase in Psalm 130 that describes "sins" (CEB), or the "record of my guilt" (Greenberg), or "iniquities" (NRSVue) as acts of bending, turning aside, twisting. What actions or turnings from what is right need to be named? What injustices need to be called out?
3. Think about a time you have experienced God's forgiveness. How would you describe it?
4. What do you think is the difference between waiting and hoping?
5. What is your experience of waiting for God?

Pause (5 minutes)

Depending on the members of your group and their interests and your time for preparation, consider assembling small seed pots, the kind that can be planted directly in the ground. Bring small pots, a bag of dirt, and seed packets, and invite those who are interested to plant seeds in their pot. Others might enjoy taking pots and seeds to plant later or to give to someone.

As participants are planting, invite response to this reflection: Think about the season of Lent we have been walking through together with this study. Think about the psalms we have been reading and studying. In what ways have you taken time to wait, to notice how God is speaking to you in and through these ancient texts? How have the spiritual practices nurtured your life of faith?

Close with a final reading of Psalm 130 and a prayer.

HOLY WEEK

Psalm 118: Thanksgiving with Palm Sunday
Psalm 116: Listening on Maundy Thursday
Psalm 22: Being Alone or Abandoned on Good Friday
Psalm 19: Hands of Easter

Preparing to Teach

This book offers chapters for each of the days of Holy Week. If you are discussing the book with a group that meets on Sunday or one other time during the week, you may not have time to focus on all four of the psalms for this week, which are to be read individually on Palm Sunday, Maundy Thursday, Good Friday, and Easter. Read over the chapters in the book and decide which one(s) will be your focus as a group, and encourage participants to continue reflecting on the psalm and chapter for each day as they move through Holy Week. Leader's guides are available for all four psalms. You could also consider meeting the week after Easter Sunday to discuss the psalm for the Easter season.

Palm Sunday/Holy Week Leader's Guide

Psalm 118: Thanksgiving

Preparing to Teach

Read over this guide, and make note of anything you need to do to get ready to teach this session. If participants are not bringing Bibles with them, have copies available so that they can follow along as the psalm is being read. Have a palm branch on the table. Here are links to two different choral versions of Psalm 118. If you wish, have them playing as people are arriving.

- https://youtu.be/OUrw4ThH-4U: Holy Spirit Catholic Church, "This Is the Day That the Lord Has Made; Let Us Rejoice and Be Glad in It."
- https://youtu.be/EbjA0hGe73k: The University of Notre Dame Folk Choir, "Reflecting on 40 Years: Psalm 118: This Is the Day (Haugen)."

Notice (10 minutes)

As people are gathering, invite them to listen to one of the choir recordings of Psalm 118. Have this question available on a screen or on a flipchart or whiteboard:

What sounds familiar to you in this psalm?

119

After receiving some responses, open with a prayer, either by you or one of the participants.

Attend (30 minutes)

- Provide a brief introduction to Psalm 118 using information that is available in the "Attend" section of the Palm Sunday chapter (p. 64). You may also show the introductory video for this chapter (found at www.wjkbooks.com/Pause). Note that this is a psalm of thanksgiving read by Jews on Passover, Shavuot, and Sukkot and is the most quoted psalm in the New Testament.
- This long psalm has three sections. It will help the discussion of the psalm by asking three people to read these sections: call to worship (vv. 1–4); voice of the individual (vv. 5–18); voice of the individual then joining with the worshiping community (vv. 19–29). Invite participants to listen for phrases that are repeated and ones that are familiar to them.
- Discuss the parts of the psalm that connect with thanksgiving and the celebration of Palm Sunday. The study gives you some background on two major themes of the psalm: God's steadfast love and God's presence in difficult times.
- Have the illustrated sheet for Palm Sunday/Holy Week/Psalm 118:24 available for everyone to see, either projected or printed (found at www.wjkbooks.com/Pause). Hear them read, and then discuss these questions:

  1. How is God described?
  2. What are the similarities and differences you notice?

Connect (15 minutes)

Have the online resource sheet with the questions for reflection and discussion printed or available for viewing on-screen. Use these questions to help participants connect their experiences with those of the psalmist:

  1. What is your experience of knowing the steadfast love of God?

2. Recall a time when you were in a tight space and saw no way out. In what ways was God present for you, inviting you into a wider or better place?
3. In what ways have your understandings about the nature of God changed over the years?
4. What words or images would you use to describe your thanksgiving to God?

Pause (5 minutes)

The practice of noticing and celebrating the ways we see God at work in the world prepares participants as they begin to move from Palm Sunday into Holy Week. As you close this time together, invite participants to take out their phones and look at the most recent photographs they have taken. Or ask them to review the pictures in their mind of the preceding week. Invite responses to these questions:

1. Who or what do you want to remember and celebrate today?
2. Where did you see God at work in our world last week?

Close this time together by inviting everyone to say together this verse from Psalm 118:24: "This is the day that the LORD has made; let us rejoice and be glad in it."

Maundy Thursday Leader's Guide

Psalm 116: Listening

Preparing to Teach

Read over this guide, and make note of anything you need to do to get ready to teach this session. If participants are not bringing Bibles with them, have copies available so that they can follow along as the psalm is being read. If you want to have participants create a prayer box for the "Pause" section of this session, you can find small paper boxes at craft stores.

Notice (10 minutes)

As people are gathering, have this question available on a screen or printed on a flipchart or whiteboard:

> What was your experience last week of really listening to some-
> one or someone listening to you?

After collecting responses, open with a prayer, either by you or one of the participants.

Attend (30 minutes)

• Before hearing Psalm 116 read, provide an introduction using information that is available in the "Attend" section of the Maundy
  Thursday chapter (p. 72). You may also show the introductory

video for this chapter (found at www.wjkbooks.com/Pause). Include how this psalm of thanksgiving is read both at Passover and in Christian worship on Maundy Thursday.

• The psalm has a simple literary structure of three sections: verses 1–2 begin the psalm with an acknowledgment of God's love; verses 3–11 describe the experiences of the psalmist; and in verses 12–19, we hear the voice of the psalmist and the promises made because of the way God has listened and acted. Ask three people to read these three sections. As they do so, invite participants to listen for the experiences of the psalm writer.

• Have the illustrated sheet for Maundy Thursday/Psalm 116:1–2 available for everyone to see, either projected or printed (found at www.wjkbooks.com/Pause). Ask a participant to read each one. Though they share some common phrasing, they provide us with rich images of how the psalmist experienced God's presence. Ask these questions:

1. How is God described?
2. What are the similarities and differences you notice?

Connect (15 minutes)

Have the online resource sheet with the questions for reflection and discussion printed or available for viewing on-screen. The image has changed from the first page. Begin this time by asking participants to reflect on what is evoked for them as they think about this illustration, this psalm, and this Maundy Thursday. Use any of these questions to help participants connect their experiences with those of the psalmist:

1. Imagine yourself at the Passover table with Jesus in the upper room. What do you think you would have heard? What question would you have asked?
2. In the upper room, Jesus invited disciples to share a meal and to receive the gift of having their feet washed. And he reminded them of a new commandment: to love. What stories do you

want to recover that testify to the ways these acts are evident today in your life, in the life of your church, or in the life of your community?

3. In what ways have you experienced God listening to your prayers? How are they similar to or different from the experiences of the speaker in this psalm?

4. In what ways are your ears open or closed to those around you?

Pause (5 minutes)

Here are two ways to conclude this session:

• Have small paper boxes and strips of paper available for each person. Invite them to think about the people who have listened to them this week and to write down their names and place them in the box. Then think about the people they have listened to, writing those names and placing them in the box. Encourage participants to keep the boxes somewhere visible where they will see them during the day and be reminded of how God listens and calls us to listen.

• Invite participants to complete this phrase: *I love the Lord because* . . .

Close with prayer.

Good Friday Leader's Guide

Psalm 22: Being Alone or Abandoned

Preparing to Teach

Read over this guide, and make note of anything you need to do to get ready to teach this session. If participants are not bringing Bibles with them, have copies available so that they can follow along as the psalm is being read. Have a candle, either real or battery-operated.

Notice (10 minutes)

As people are gathering, have this question available on a screen or printed on a flipchart or whiteboard:

> Think about a time in your life when you felt most alone or abandoned. Was that a time when you felt separated from family, friend, even God?

As you begin, light the candle and open with prayer.

Attend (30 minutes)

• Before hearing Psalm 22 read, provide a brief introduction to the psalm using information that is available in the "Attend" section of the Good Friday chapter (p. 80). You may also show the introductory video for this chapter (found at www.wjkbooks .com/Pause). Psalm 22 has a rich history for both Jews and

Christians. The literary form is an individual song of complaint or lament. It was probably written before the Babylonian exile and the destruction of the temple in Jerusalem. A lament psalm has these basic elements: address to God, specific complaints, a plea for help, and an affirmation by the psalmist that God will hear. According to Mark and Matthew, Jesus uttered the first words of this psalm at his crucifixion. The psalm is traditionally read during Good Friday services.

• Invite participants to take turns reading the psalm in these sections: verses 1–5; 6–18; 19–22; and 23–31.
• Discuss these questions:

1. What is the lament?
2. Where do you see the writer affirming connections with the community?
3. What is the writer saying about God?

• Have the illustrated sheet for Good Friday/Psalm 22 available for everyone to see, either projected or printed (found at www .wjkbooks.com/Pause). Hear them read, and discuss these questions:

1. How is the situation of the psalmist described?
2. How is the plea to God expressed?
3. Where do you see possible connections in the psalm to help you understand Jesus' suffering on the cross?

Connect (15 minutes)

Have the online resource sheet with the questions for reflection and discussion printed or available for viewing on-screen. Use these questions to help participants connect their experiences with those of the psalmist:

1. What is your lament, your "loud groan"?
2. When was a time you felt distant from God's presence in your life?

3. Whom do you know who struggles with feeling alone, separated either from God or from a community of support?
4. In what ways is God making God's face visible to you, especially in times of trial?

Pause (5 minutes)

This psalm provides a voice of lament, but the writer turns to the community of which he is a part. Close the session in community by asking participants to name the laments that are on their hearts this day as they meditate on Good Friday. For the closing prayer, read verses 25–31.

Easter Leader's Guide

Psalm 19: Hands

Preparing to Teach

Read over this guide, and make note of anything you need to do to get ready to teach this session. If participants are not bringing Bibles with them, have copies available so that they can follow along as the psalm is being read. A vase of spring flowers will add a note of celebration for this Easter Sunday.

Notice (10 minutes)

As people are gathering, have this question available on a screen or printed on a flipchart or whiteboard:

> What are some of your favorite memories of Easter celebrations either at church, or at home, or in your community?

After collecting responses, open with prayer, either by you or from one of the participants.

Attend (30 minutes)

• Before hearing Psalm 19 read, provide an introduction to how the psalmist is expressing an affirmation for the ways God is revealed. Use information that is available in the "Attend" section of the Easter chapter (p. 90). You may also show the introductory video for this chapter (found at www.wjkbooks.com/Pause).

- The psalm has a simple literary structure with three sections: how God is known in creation (vv. 1–6); how God is known in the goodness of the law (vv. 7–10); and a confession of failure and a plea for God's presence (vv. 11–13). Ask three people to read these three sections. Invite everyone to read together verse 14.
- The psalm provides a great way to reflect on how the original audience would have seen God's acts in the world through creation and law (*torah*). They did not experience laws as restrictive but rather as a comforting reminder of God's presence and God's faithful actions.
- Have the illustrated sheet for Easter/Psalm 19 available for everyone to see (found at www.wjkbooks.com/Pause). Hear them read, and then discuss these questions:

    1. What are the similarities and differences you notice?
    2. Which descriptions of God's handiwork are you most drawn to?

Connect (15 minutes)

Have the online resource sheet with the questions for reflection and discussion printed or available for viewing on-screen. Use these questions to help participants connect their experiences with those of the psalmist:

    1. What do you notice in creation that reveals God's handiwork?
    2. What connections can you see between Psalm 19 and Easter?
    3. In what ways does your life story reveal God's presence in your life?
    4. Where are your hands needed in the work of your church, your community, the world?

Pause (5 minutes)

Close with the breath prayer that is suggested in the study using the last verse of the psalm. Start by saying each phrase below out loud. Read the questions to participants, and pause for reflection.

- *"Let the words of my mouth . . ."* Think about the words you have said this day either to yourself or in conversation. Were there

any that could have been hurtful? What words were comforting? What words needed to be said to address injustice?

- *". . . and the meditation of my heart . . ."* Listen to your heart and
  the things that have been silently and maybe not so silently
  waiting there. What are you contemplating or meditating on? Is
  it a person, a situation?
- *". . . be acceptable to you, O LORD, my rock and my redeemer."* In what
  ways could your words or meditations change so that God
  would see them as pleasing or helpful or useful in the world?
  The psalmist affirms God as rock and redeemer. What words
  would you use to describe God's presence in your life?

Now try saying these verses as a breath prayer. Guide participants to
take a deep breath as you read the first phrase, breathe out with the
second phrase, and so on.

Close the session and study with a final prayer.

Notes

Introduction

1. Walter Brueggemann and William H. Bellinger Jr., *Psalms*, New Cambridge Bible Commentary (New York: Cambridge University Press, 2014), 2.

First Week of Lent

1. Konrad Schaefer, *Psalms*, Berit Olam: Studies in Hebrew Narrative and Poetry, ed. David W. Cotter (Collegeville, MN: Liturgical Press, 2001), 63.
2. Walter Brueggemann and William H. Bellinger Jr., *Psalms*, New Cambridge Bible Commentary (New York: Cambridge University Press, 2014), 133.

Second Week of Lent

1. Lindsay P. Armstrong, "Pastoral Perspective on Psalm 27," in *Feasting on the Word: Preaching the Revised Common Lectionary, Year C, Volume 2*, ed. David L. Bartlett and Barbara Brown Taylor (Louisville, KY: Westminster John Knox Press, 2009), 58.

Third Week of Lent

1. Robin Gallaher Branch, "Exegetical Perspective on Psalm 63:1-8," in *Feasting on the Word: Preaching the Revised Common Lectionary, Year C, Volume 2*, ed. David L. Bartlett and Barbara Brown Taylor (Louisville, KY: Westminster John Knox Press, 2009), 83.
2. J. Clinton McCann Jr., commentary on Psalm 63:1–8, in *Connections: A Lectionary Commentary for Preaching and Worship, Year C, Volume 2*, ed. Joel B. Green, Thomas G. Long, Luke A. Powery, and Cynthia L. Rigby (Louisville, KY: Westminster John Knox Press, 2018), 67.

3. Richard C. Stern, "Homiletical Perspective on Psalm 63:1–8," in *Feasting on the Word, Year C, Volume 2*, 85.

Fourth Week of Lent

1. Robert Alter, *The Hebrew Bible*, vol. 3, *The Writings* (New York: W. W. Norton, 2019), 70.
2. Kent M. French, "Exegetical Perspective on Psalm 23," in *Feasting on the Word: Preaching the Revised Common Lectionary, Year B, Volume 2*, ed. David L. Bartlett and Barbara Brown Taylor (Louisville, KY: Westminster John Knox Press, 2008), 439.
3. Walter Brueggemann and William H. Bellinger Jr., *Psalms*, New Cambridge Bible Commentary (New York: Cambridge University Press, 2014), 124.
4. Barbara Hamm, "Come to the Table of Grace," Hope Publishing, 2008.
5. Kendall Vanderslice, "On Stores at the Table," *Edible Theology* (blog), *The Weekly Digest*, April 30, 2023.

Fifth Week of Lent

1. Nancy deClaissé-Walford, *Psalms, Books 4–5*, Wisdom Commentary (Collegeville, MN: Liturgical Press, 2020), 171.
2. DeClaissé-Walford, *Psalms, Books 4–5*, 211.
3. DeClaissé-Walford, 213.
4. Nancy deClaissé-Walford, "Commentary on Psalm 130," Working Preacher, March 29, 2020, https://www.workingpreacher.org/commentaries/revised-common-lectionary/fifth-sunday-in-lent/commentary-on-psalm-130-7.
5. Pamela Greenberg, *The Complete Psalms: The Book of Prayer Songs in a New Translation* (New York: Bloomsbury, 2010), 286.

Palm Sunday/Holy Week

1. Walter Brueggemann and William H. Bellinger Jr., *Psalms*, New Cambridge Bible Commentary (New York: Cambridge University Press, 2014), 509.
2. Brueggemann and Bellinger, *Psalms*, 509.
3. Stephen Montgomery, "Pastoral Perspective on Psalm 118," in *Feasting on the Word: Preaching the Revised Common Lectionary, Year B, Volume 2*, ed. David L. Bartlett and Barbara Brown Taylor (Louisville, KY: Westminster John Knox Press, 2008), 146.

Reflection for Maundy Thursday

1. Robert Alter, *The Hebrew Bible*, vol. 3, *The Writings* (Ketuvim) (New York: W. W. Norton, 2019), 274.
2. David J. Wood, "Pastoral Perspective on Psalm 116," in *Feasting on the Word: Preaching the Revised Common Lectionary, Year B, Volume 2*, ed. David L. Bartlett and Barbara Brown Taylor (Louisville, KY: Westminster John Knox Press, 2008), 268.

3. Atler, *The Hebrew Bible*, 274.
4. Konrad Schaefer, *Psalms*, Berit Olam: Studies in Hebrew Narrative and Poetry, ed. David W. Cotter (Collegeville, MN: Liturgical Press, 2001), 285.

Reflection for Good Friday

1. Esther Menn, "No Ordinary Lament: Relecture and the Identity of the Distressed in Psalm 22," *Harvard Theological Review* 93, no. 4 (October 2000): 2.
2. Walter Brueggemann and William H. Bellinger Jr., *Psalms*, New Cambridge Bible Commentary (New York: Cambridge University Press, 2014), 119.
3. Adam Jacob Berkovitz, "Jewish and Christian Exegetical Controversy in Late Antiquity: The Case of Psalm 22 and the Esther Narrative," in *Ancient Readers and Their Scriptures: Engaging the Hebrew Bible in Early Judaism and Christianity*, ed. Garrick V. Allen and John Anthony Dunne, Ancient Judaism and Early Christianity 107 (Leiden: Brill), 222-39 (239).
4. Amy-Jill Levine and Marc Zvi Brettler, *The Bible with and without Jesus: How Jews and Christians Read the Same Stories Differently* (New York: HarperOne, 2020), 379.
5. Levine and Brettler, *Bible with and without Jesus*, 379.
6. Ellen F. Davis, *Getting Involved with God: Rediscovering the Old Testament* (Boston: Cowley Publications, 2001), 15.

Reflection for Easter

1. Mark Stanger, "Exegetical Perspective on Psalm 19," in *Feasting on the Word: Preaching the Revised Common Lectionary, Year B, Volume 2*, ed. David L. Bartlett and Barbara Brown Taylor (Louisville, KY: Westminster John Knox Press, 2008), 81.
2. Konrad Schaefer, *Psalms*, Berit Olam: Studies in Hebrew Narrative and Poetry, ed. David W. Cotter (Collegeville, MN: Liturgical Press, 2001), 47.
3. Schaefer, *Psalms*, 45.
4. Schaefer, 47.
5. Stanger, "Exegetical Perspective on Psalm 19," 85.

Printed in the USA
CPSIA information can be obtained
at www.ICGtesting.com
LVHW022304070224
771286LV00036B/1421